amazing SNOOKER TRICK SHOTS

Secrets from the best!

JOHN VIRGO

WP

Published by:

WP Wilkinson Publishing Pty Ltd

ACN 006 042 173
Level 4, 2 Collins Street
Melbourne, Vic 3000
Tel: +613 9654 5446
www.wilkinsonpublishing.com.au

National Library of Australia Cataloguing-in-Publication data:

Author: Virgo, John.

Title: Amazing snooker trick shots : secrets from the best! / John Virgo.

ISBN: 9781921804670 (pbk.)

Subjects: Snooker.

               Snooker--Handbooks, manuals, etc.

Dewey Number: 794.73

Layout Design: Chris Georgiou

CONTENTS

INTRODUCTION FROM JIM DAVIDSON

A few years ago an old friend of mine said I should meet this bloke who could teach me a trick or two. Summing up every ounce of South-East London modesty I said "You must be joking". I've been known to pull a few tricks myself over the years, but who was this geezer who could teach me anything?

I was introduced to John Virgo - a man, I was to discover, who had a smile as wide as Steve Davis's wallet. If ever there was a man born to entertain, it was the big J.V. From the minute I met him, his droll, laid-back sense of humour had me grinning from ear to ear.

Straight away, I nick-named him "Grumpy". One night I saw him standing stoney-faced outside his local pub in Surrey. "Oi, J.V.!" I called, "why aren't you inside the pub?"

"It's happy hour," was his reply.

Seriously though, John has forged himself a whole new career in showbusiness, having been one of the most successful and engaging players on the professional snooker circuit. I can tell you that he has even taught ME a few trick shots, and I am to snooker what Alex Higgins was to diplomacy! During rehearsals for *Big Break* he always had everybody spellbound and in stitches as he executed each new trick - usually accompanied by a new gag.

I will let you into a secret about J.V. His world revolves around the game to such an extent that he went on a diet eating only snooker balls! When he asked me why he had not lost any weight I told him, "You're not eating enough greens mate!"

And now for John's book of snooker trick shots. I'm sure you'll have lots of fun with it. Apparently there's some in here that even I could do!

JOHN VIRGO'S INTRODUCTION

A lot of people have told me how much they enjoyed the trick shot section I did every week on *Big Break*. I was inspired by a snooker player called Jackie Rea who used to visit snooker halls in the Sixties. After playing a few frames he would do some trick shots and I thought he was great. Everyone, it seems to me, finds them entertaining.

Well, with the aid of this book, you too can amaze your friends by performing a hundred different shots, some of which I have done on *Big Break*. There is a mixture of standard classics, my own inventions and variations. I'm sure that you will be able to come up with your own variations after working your way through this book. If you think they're good enough, why not write to tell me about them via my website: www.johnvirgo.com. Who knows? We might get enough for a second book of one hundred shots!

All of the trick shots here have been tried and tested. There are three sections – for Absolute Beginners, Trickier Trick Shots and Try 'em If You Dare! But if you are a complete beginner you should be able to do all (or almost all!) the shots by slowly working your way through the book.

The things you will learn in the first section will come in useful for some of the trickier stuff later on. So get a feel for the cue, the angles and pace first, before rushing to the end.

Some of the shots won't work first time. Be patient because many will take a lot of practice, not just in hitting the ball properly, but in setting up the shot so that you have the right angles.

Stick with it, I promise it will be worthwhile in the end. Most importantly of all, enjoy yourself. This is a fun book.

Let's start with a few basic principles . . .

BASIC TECHNIQUES

THE LOOP BRIDGE

Quite a few of the shots are best played using a loop bridge in which the thumb and index finger form a loop for the cue to pass through and rest on the knuckle of the middle finger.

It will help you to keep the cue down, which is particularly useful when you need to play with a lot of follow-through.

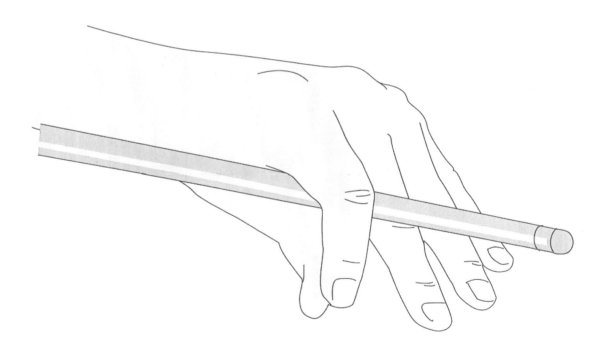

A PLANT

An example of a plant is where there are two balls touching or nearly touching and you hit the cue ball onto the first ball in order to move the second where you want it. You can have a five ball plant in which the first four will move the end ball. It's a combination of each ball hitting the other.

It works on the same principle as Newton's Cradle.

If you hit one ball against a row of four then one ball moves off the end. If you hit two, then two will move and so on.

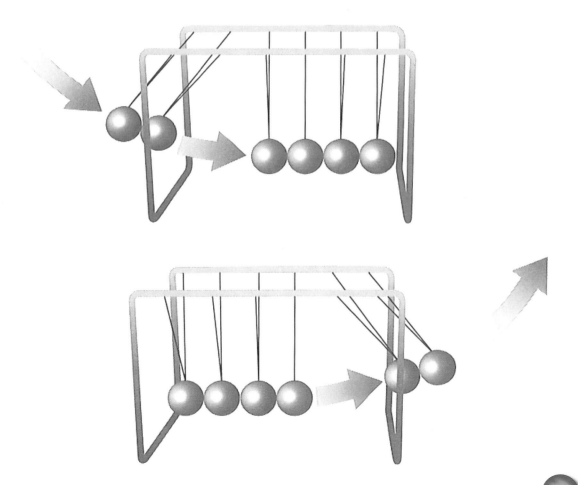

A CANNON

Is when you strike the cue ball to hit one ball and it moves across to hit another.

CLOCK FACE

For simplification I have used the clock face format to specify where you should strike the cue ball. For example, instead of saying hit with 'bottom', I will say 'six o'clock'. 'Top' is 'twelve o'clock' and so on.

If you hit the cue ball at twelve o'clock you get top spin. This gives the ball more pace. You might, for example need to pot the black and run round off two cushions for a red.

At six o'clock you get backspin, causing the cue ball to screw back towards you after it has made contact with the object ball.

At three o'clock you get right-hand side spin which can be useful, for instance, if you want the ball to hug the side cushion on its way into the pocket. And at nine o'clock you get left-hand spin.

The more follow-through you put on a ball, the more spin you will get, which will be required for certain shots.

POSTURE

Get your chin low over the cue. The main thing is to have a good, balanced stance. With your hand on the table and feet spread, you form a tripod. If you've got that balance and you push the cue through straight, then there's no shot, really, that you should not be able to play.

Feel ready to try your first trick shot? Let's go then.

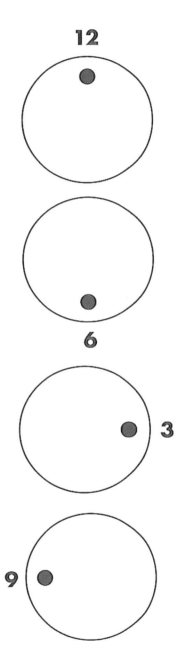

Part 1

For
ABSOLUTE
BEGINNERS

"Starting out is always fun…"

KISS THE PINK

This is a fun one to get you in the mood. You have the black on the blue spot and the white and pink as shown in the diagram. Then you announce to your audience that you are going to play a screw shot which will pot the black and kiss the pink into the bottom pocket.

It looks impossible, but what you do is hit the cue ball at six o'clock and pot the black, pick up the pink, kiss it and put it into the pocket! The white is placed at a slight angle so that it doesn't screw back into the middle pocket.

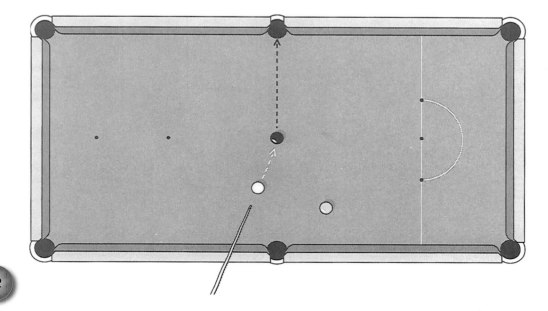

TWO FOR THE PRICE OF ONE 2

Here we demonstrate how you can pot two balls together by playing with bottom. The backspin imparted has the same effect as if you were playing two balls against two.

Put two red balls over the pocket, in a direct line, touching, and the cue ball on the blue spot. Strike it at six o'clock and the reds will both go into the pocket. This is a very good shot to practice because you play it with follow through. If you strike the cue ball in the middle you will see that only one ball will pot.

• **One of the first shots people learn is with the triangle because we are all fascinated at the thought of potting the six colours all in one shot. Somebody discovered that it could be done like this . . .**

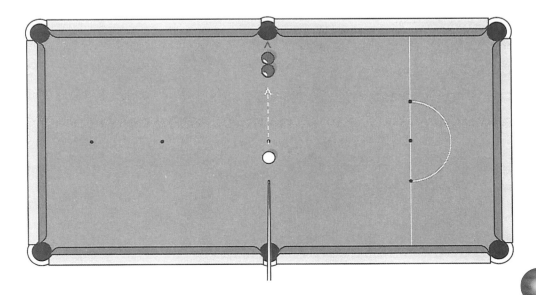

3 BERMUDA TRIANGLE

Guaranteed to impress. Inform your audience that you can pot all six coloured balls in one shot. Whilst your friends are puzzling over how you are going to accomplish this, you can add that they will go down in order – yellow, green, brown, blue, pink and black.

Let them have a try. When they've failed, line up the balls as shown, then produce the triangle and lay it down with the point touching the black ball. You then hit the cue ball hard at the triangle and knock all the balls into the pocket.

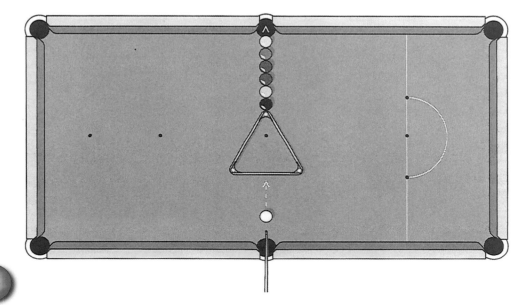

RETURN OF THE BERMUDA TRIANGLE

To make it look better you could put the black ball over the other middle pocket and if you play the cue ball just below centre, at six o'clock, it will rebound off the triangle and knock the black in.

• **But it's easy to knock six coloured balls in with one shot. Later we'll be showing you how difficult it is to knock just one ball in!**

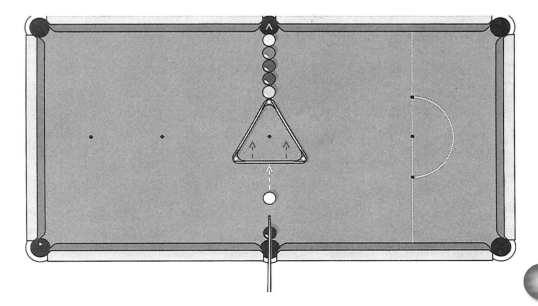

5 KNOCK ON WOOD

Here you put the triangle point on the edge of the middle pocket, put the black in the middle and say you are going to hit the black into the pocket. You then hit the cue ball at the triangle, the point juts over the pocket and the ball drops in.

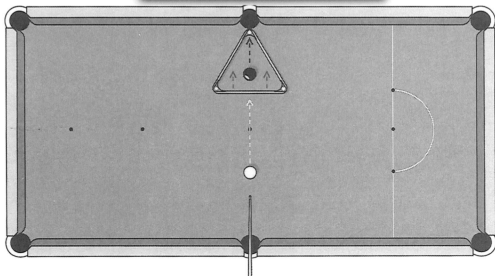

IMPOSSIBLE REDS

This time place two reds over both middle pockets and another red and the cue ball in a line. Declare that you are about to pot three reds in one shot.

Don't produce the triangle until people have tried to work out how they would do it. Then place it over the red ball, as shown, and the shot is the same principle as with shot four. Strike the ball below centre, two will go in, the cue ball rebounds and knocks the other red in.

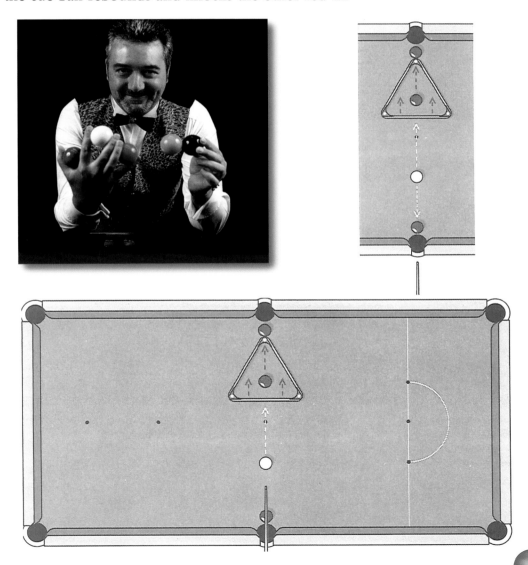

7 TRICKLE TEASER

Kids love this one. Boast that you can pot seven balls at once and then simply lay two cues as shown and run the balls down them into the middle pocket. You can use as many balls as you like!

- **You can make a trick shot more interesting with your style and patter, creating an act, much like a magician does with a card trick. But by now you will have realised that it's what you don't say that's important! Just announce what you are going to do but don't give any idea how you are going to do it.**

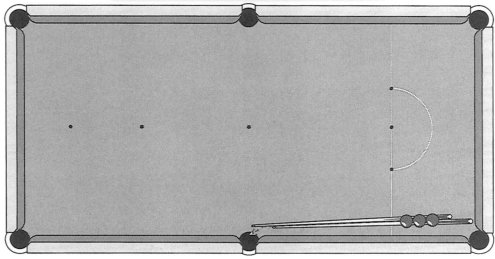

COLLAPSING SHOT

Jim Davidson taught me this shot on *Big Break*. He said it was a good way of winning a pint from your pals if you're a bit strapped for cash!

Put two reds against the top cushion and the black perched above them, actually *on top* of the cushion. With the cue ball at the other end of the table you bet a pint that you will hit the black without touching the reds.

Slowly knock the cue ball up the table. Walk to the other end and, as it approaches, bang the top of the cushion so that the black falls through the two reds and makes contact with the white. Voila! Mine's a lager!

" A lot of people ask me what Jim Davidson is like at snooker. I can only answer with one word – terrible!"

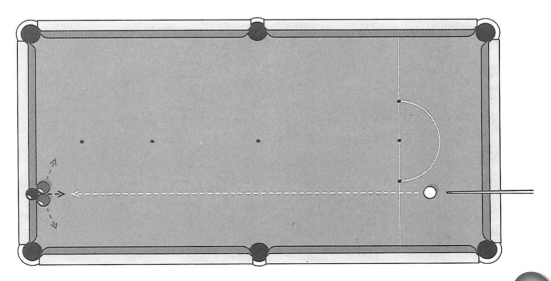

⑨ SNOOKER CHEAT

This one really is a *trick shot*. It's all an illusion, and the quicker you play it, the more impressive it looks. Set up the white, a red and the black in line with the corner pocket. If you gently hit the cue ball it will touch the red. Then slightly raise your cue as you follow through and hit the black directly, powering it into the corner pocket. This will look brilliant with a bit of practice.

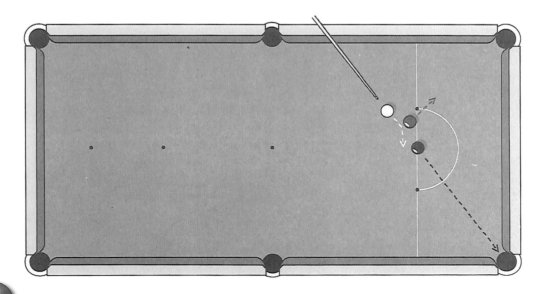

SNOOKER CHEAT PART 2

A variation on Shot 9 is to place a pink in between the pocket and black. You can then pot the pink by hitting it with the black, which you have struck directly with the cue.

You will know when you're getting good at this type of shot because people will ask you how to do it. Like all good magicians, you shouldn't tell them. Let them figure it out for themselves.

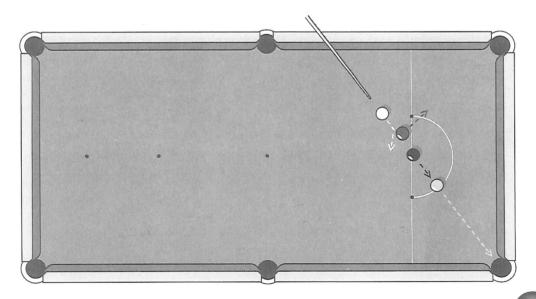

PEAS IN THE POD

With this one we're trying to pot the black but you've got to hit the pink first.

Place two reds at an angle by the middle pocket, with the pink and black behind. All four balls should be touching – you may not need to experiment with the cluster's position.

Strike the cue ball at around nine o'clock to hit the pink on the right hand side. The pink hits the first red which knocks the other so that these three balls disperse. And, having played slightly on the right-hand side of the pink, there's a delayed reaction as the black makes its way into the middle pocket.

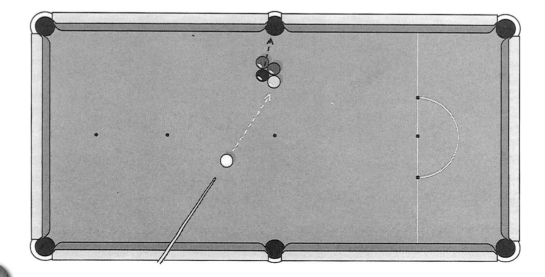

THE COIN IN THE GLASS 12

The classic Coin In The Glass shot looks difficult but it's quite easy once you've practiced for a while and discovered how hard you should hit the cue ball. And it's a real crowd pleaser.

You need a squat glass – a whisky tumbler is ideal – and a 5p coin (it used to be a sixpence). Put the coin just on the edge of the cushion – but not overlapping – and the glass behind it, on the wood. With the cue ball in the middle of the table, hit it hard at the cushion and the bounce will cause the penny to flip up into the glass.

•   **All tables vary. On some you have to strike the ball harder than on others. With all of these trick shots, hit the ball with a good pace the first time and then make alterations wherever necessary.**

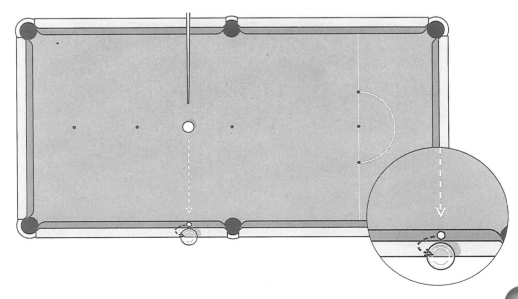

THE PINT POT SHOT 13

Whilst you're at the glass cabinet . . . get a straight pint pot. And then pot the pint! It's a shot I've done on *Big Break*.

Place the glass against the side of the cushion. Press the cue on top, give it a shove and the glass will roll in an arc into the middle pocket. You'll have to judge exactly where to place it. The most important thing of all is to make sure the glass is empty!

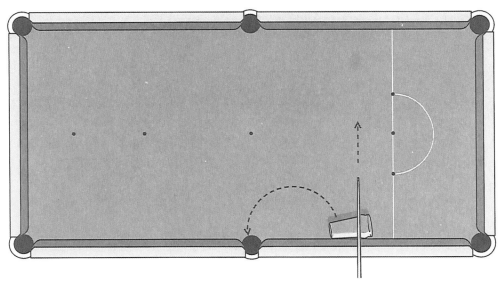

14 AROUND THE ANGLES

This is a good one to practice. Place the black ball on the pink spot with the triangle resting on it. You then strike the cue ball to send it off three cushions and knock the black into the triangle.

You can strike it full in the face but I'd personally play the cue ball at three o'clock, so that you get some right-hand side.

It's just enabling you to get a feel of the cue for some of the trickier shots we'll be doing later on, as well as becoming familiar with the angles. It will also get you used to hitting the ball harder because there will be some shots where you will really need to give it a whack!

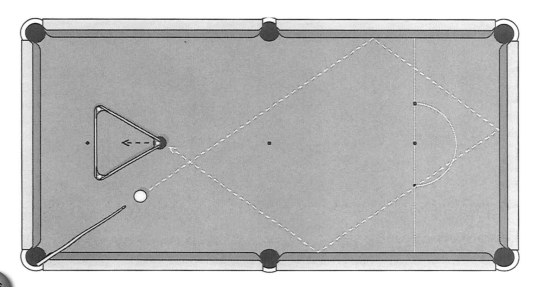

NEWTON'S CRADLE

This shot demonstrates the Newton's Cradle effect that we explained at the beginning. Put a line of reds and the pink and black along the cushion. The blue ball is on the end, at an angle. Place a spare red near the middle pocket and the white and red together as shown.

The pink and blue balls have to get out of the way in order to pot the black in the middle pocket so you push the white and red together, which moves the pink and blue balls to one side. The pink takes the blue away and the black will then run along and go in off the red.

It's really just a matter of striking the ball with a fair amount of pace for the shot to work.

• Push shots are illegal in snooker but we're not concerning ourselves with the legalities of the game in this book.

• **An interesting point to remember is that all tables are brushed and ironed from the baulk end to the top end. So the nap of the cloth is towards the black spot which means that a ball will hug the top cushion more closely than it will at the baulk end.**

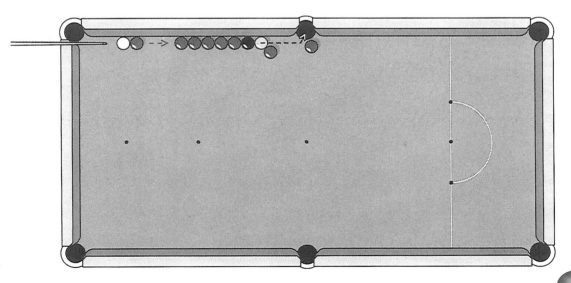

16 SPIT SHOT

Tricky at first, but you'll have licked it by the end! Set the balls up as shown, with the black and red touching each other against the bottom cushion and another red touching the black at an angle. Then ask a friend to pot the black into the left corner pocket.

It might look like the black would pot if a plant is played but, no matter how many times he tries, the black will pull away from the cushion. So, whilst he's scratching his head, set the balls up again and, in doing so, slyly wet your thumb with your tongue, and wipe it on the part of the red that's going to be touching the black.

If you now play the shot, the black will go in because the saliva will cause the balls to stick together for a while, holding the black onto the cushion so that it can pot.

For these next three push shots I advise you to use the loop bridge that I mentioned earlier, to make sure the cue stays horizontal with the table.

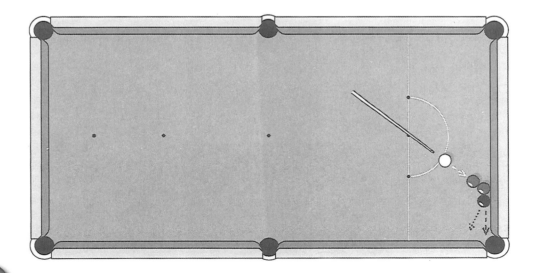

EIGHT BALL FRENZY 17

The cue ball is at the front of a row of reds in line with the middle pocket. The black ball has another two reds on the end of it, the last one at an angle.

Strike the cue ball full in the face, the front reds move out of the way and the black pots.

Take some care in setting up these shots. You'll probably need to try them out a few times before you get the balls placed accurately.

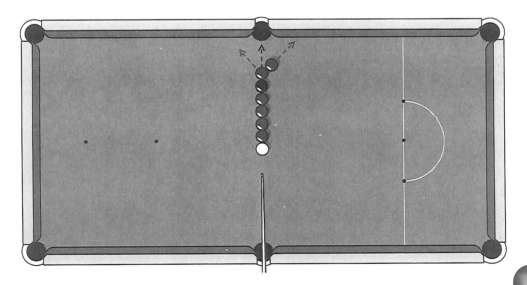

18 CUMBERLAND GAP

Form a lozenge shape in the middle of the table with two rows of reds and the black positioned as shown, all slightly spaced apart. Place the cue ball at the front and then remove one of the balls to leave a gap. There should now be on the table ten red balls, the black and the white.

You are now going to pot the black in the right middle pocket. The gap causes a ball delay so that if you hit the first red, the unbroken side of reds will make contact with the two end balls (which are closer together than the others), moving them away, and the black will then pot in the centre pocket.

It sounds complicated but it's an easy shot. All you have to do is hit down the middle, striking the cue ball full in the face.

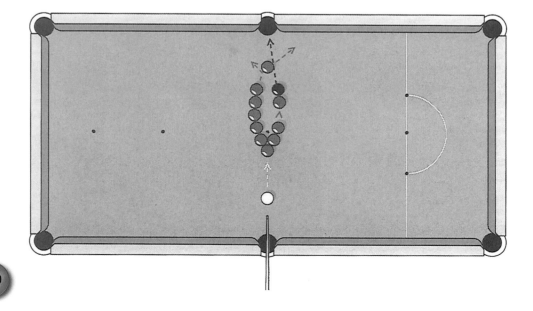

THE WALLED PRISON 19

Form another lozenge shape with the reds, but this time all the balls are either touching or almost touching (judge for yourself what works best). The black is directly in line with the middle right pocket. So too is the white at the other end and the pink in the middle.

This time your audience might be expecting you to pot the black but you surprise them by saying that you are going to pot the pink.

With the cue ball touching the front two reds, play it with plenty of follow through. The black ball is there to knock the end two reds away and the black will shift too, making way for the pink to pot.

It doesn't matter if any other balls go into pockets in the process. Everyone will be thinking, 'How on earth is he going to pot the pink?' That's the trick. It looks like it can't escape its walled prison, but it can.

• **Now for some fun shots with the triangle which will teach you how to make a ball jump. It's important to put down a spare square of baize when playing these shots so that you don't tear the table.**

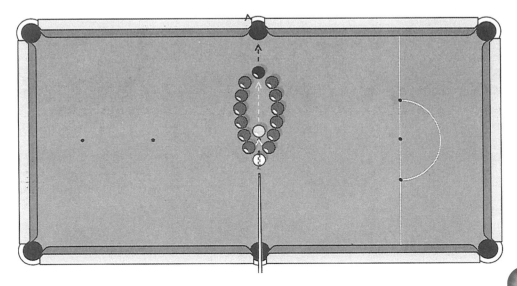

20 THROUGH THE KEYHOLE

Stand the triangle up on its base, near the blue spot. Put the black ball over the middle pocket and by striking down on the cue ball it will jump through the triangle and knock the black in.

It looks difficult but actually it's the easiest thing in the world to get a ball to bounce. Instead of holding the cue straight, you bring the end up, strike down on the cue ball and that will cause it to jump off the table.

- **Don't forget to keep your cue chalked.**

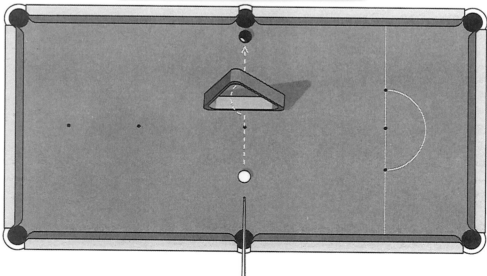

DAMBUSTERS

Barnes Wallace taught me this one. If you want to be really clever you can put another triangle mid-way between the first and the black ball. Then jump the cue ball through the first, as before, it bounces and jumps through the second, knocking the black into the pocket.

You strike it exactly the same way as you did in the last shot. The ball only has to come a little way off the table. Don't try to hit the light bulb! It's very simple. A contestant did it on *Big Break*.

• **Later on we'll be showing you some shots where you've really got to get the ball in the air! But it's basically the same principle – just striking down on the ball.**

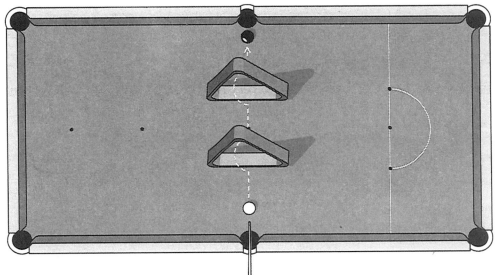

22 DON'T PUSH ME!

If only you could get away with this shot in a frame of snooker!

The black ball is hard on the cushion with the white touching it in front. Say, 'I'll pot the black'. Then *push* the white at 2 o'clock. The black sinks into the cushion and that bit of right-hand side will cause the white to move over fractionally to right of the black, which keeps it on the cushion so that it will go into the pocket.

* **All these shots can be done by a beginner. It's just a case of getting a feel for them.**

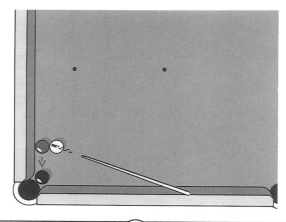

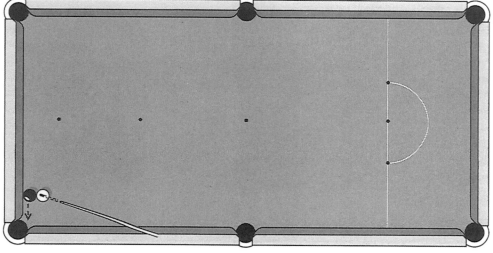

HANDY FOR SOME 23

If you've ever cuffed somebody around the ear then you'll already have a feel for this one!

Put the black over the middle right pocket, the red against the cushion on the opposite side, with the white in front.

Now say that you are going to pot the black with the cue ball. And, with the palm of your hand, hit the top of the red into the nearest cushion which will put top-spin on the ball. It back-spins off cushion, knocking the white across the table to pot the black.

There's only a little bit of red showing so you've got to be accurate, but with a bit of practice it will become easy.

If you do it quickly, people will naturally assume that you have hit the white ball. Let them try it and they will cuff the wrong one, which is hopeless.

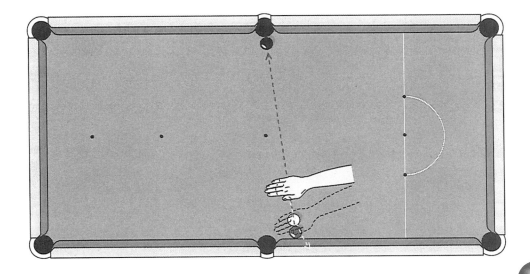

24 THE MATCH WINNER

This is a good one to become familiar with because it's a situation that can arise in the game of snooker as you are finishing off the colours.

Place the pink against the top cushion, with the black touching it behind. The white is also in line. Pot the black. It looks like it won't go but if you play the cue ball at six o'clock, hitting the black just slightly left of full in the face, it will drop into the pocket.

To play the shots in this book you have to strike the cue ball correctly in a variety of ways. Side-spin, back-spin and top-spin are all things that you use in a frame of snooker. So, as well as being fun shots, they are also good practice for the game itself.

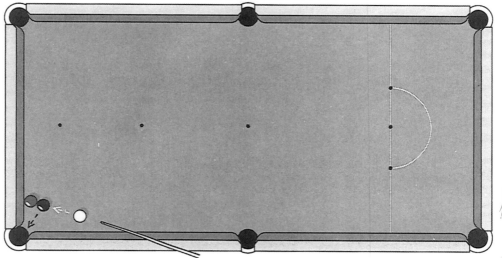

HARD REVERSE

The idea with this one is to pot the black in the bottom left corner pocket. White is tight on the top cushion. Black in front of it about an inch away. And there's a red placed near the bottom pocket to give it a nudge in, if necessary.

Strike down on the white at about twelve o'clock (you can't hit it any lower because the black is in the way). It's like the hand shot, number 23. The white is buried into the cushion, flicks back onto the black which zooms down the table into the corner pocket.

You can place a ball near the pocket (or a slanting cue) for any shot which, in effect, makes the opening wider, and so makes the pot easier. Then, when you become proficient, try it without this aid.

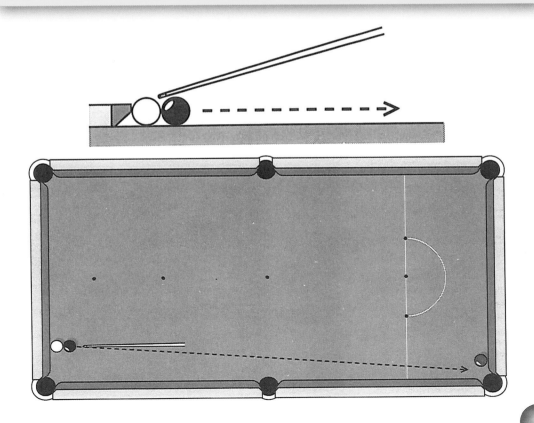

26 PENDULUM SHOT

Place four reds on the table as shown. Say that you can pot all four balls.

Then get the rest and place it on the table between the middle pockets. Nudge one into the middle right pocket with the handle, slide back to knock the left one in with the 'X'. Then, using that as a pivot, swing first to left, then to right, knocking both balls into the corner pockets. Announce, 'One, two, three, four,' as you do so.

These are shots in which you obviously don't reveal the answer until you've actually done it. Don't forget your patter. It's down to you to make each trick as entertaining as possible.

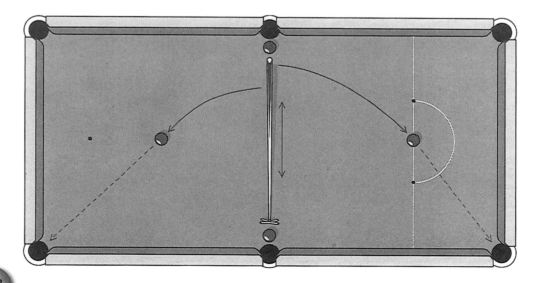

*Now how do we put
these two pieces of wood
together?*

27 POCKET THE DIFFERENCE

This is one of my favourites. Confidently declare that you are going to pot the three balls in three different pockets.

You have a red ball over both of the top corner pockets. A cue, flush against the cushion, with its tip touching the right ball and another cue alongside, touching the left ball. The white is just behind the black spot.

Hit the cue ball hard, straight down the line of spots. It rebounds off the end cushion, hits the cues, which knock in the reds, the white jumps off the table, you catch it and stick it in your trouser pocket!

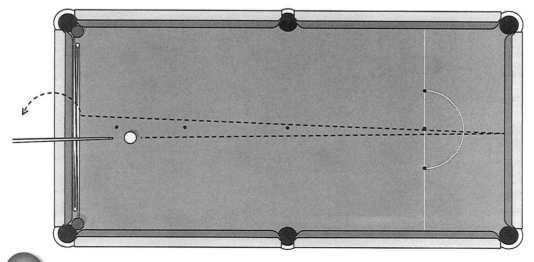

RASPBERRY RIPPLE 28

This looks effective but it's an easy shot to play. With the black ball over the top corner pocket, place a line of reds nearby, just over a ball's width away from the side cushion. Play the white from somewhere around the green spot. And the idea is to pot the black with some razzmatazz.

You play the cue ball against the cushion first, at two o'clock, to give it a bit of top and side-spin, and it has a ripple effect on the reds. They clatter away like a machine gun whilst the cue ball is held onto the cushion to pot the black. The more reds you can move away the better it will look.

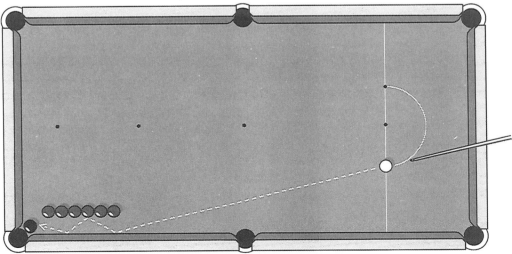

29 STRAWBERRY RIPPLE

This is a slightly different version of Shot 28 which I played on *Big Break*. You extend the reds up to the top cushion and play the white down the table. It rebounds off two sides and, as it approaches the third, you walk to the side of the table, place your cue along the cushion, the white hits it and is guided along the reds and onto the black.

At first it looks a very difficult shot but, with a bit of cheating, anything is possible!

"Jackie Rea used to be known as the Clown Prince of snooker when I watched him playing trick shots in the Sixties. He was a cheeky Irish chappie and had a good comedy routine. He also did impressions of his fellow professional players and that stuck with me."

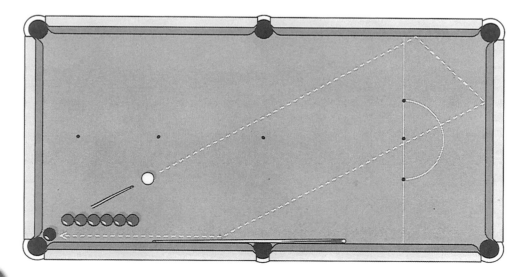

IN THE PINK

This is basically a billiard shot. If you can master this it will be useful for some shots in the 'Try 'Em if You Dare' section, towards the end of the book!

Put the pink on the blue spot with the black in front, touching.

The cue ball is played from somewhere between the green and brown spots. Strike it in the centre to hit the pink on the right-hand side and the pink will run into the middle left pocket.

We're potting the pink with this one because, once again, it's a situation that could arise in snooker. With the pink down, who's to say that the black won't have rolled over a pocket for an easy pot to win a frame?

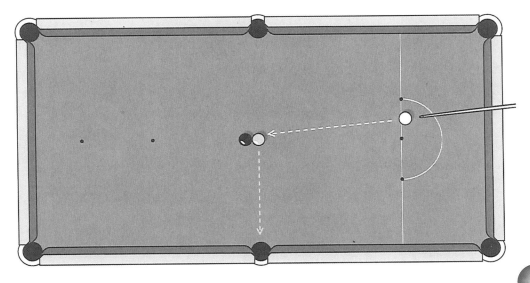

When I turned professional in 1976, my first job was doing the Butlins Holiday Camps in Skegness and Clacton-on-Sea.

The camp at Skegness was their biggest – when it was at full capacity it held over 10,000 holiday makers.

To say that the snooker tables weren't very good would be an understatement. The only way to leave the customers entertained was doing trick shots. The sports hall at Skegness consisted of 32 dart lanes, 20 table tennis tables, 10 air hockey tables and 25 snooker tables.

Needless to say not everyone was watching my exhibition. Ping pong balls kept flying across where I was performing. I had a Red Coat assisting me and when I got to the trick shot stage he had to explain what shot I was going to play, but the only way he could be heard above the noise was to use a loud hailer. It lost a little in translation, and I was really under pressure for the tricks to work first time!

SEE YOU LATER

Here's a similar shot to Shot 30 to where you pot two balls in the middle pocket.

Place the black just below the green spot and the white behind. Then produce a cue and slant it, as shown, towards the pocket. Play the white with plenty of bottom at seven o'clock. It will pot the white down one side of the cue, send the black towards the left cushion, to bounce off and roll down the other side of the cue to pot in the same pocket.

Top player Martin Clark made an impressive winning team with this contestant on Big Break. Martin's only unfulfilled ambition now is to play for Wolves.

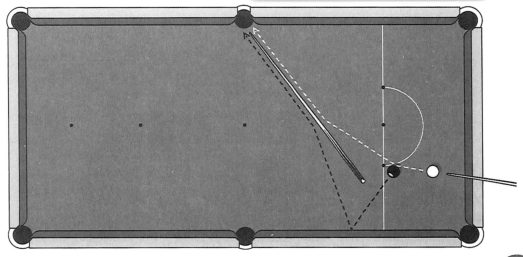

32 DISAPPEARING SHOT

This is a nice, clean shot. A classic, too. Three balls on the table and all go down.

Place the black on the pink spot with the pink ball touching it at an angle in line with the left corner pocket. Play the cue ball from between the brown and yellow spots to hit the black. The pink and black will pot in opposite corners and the white follows the line of pink into the pocket.

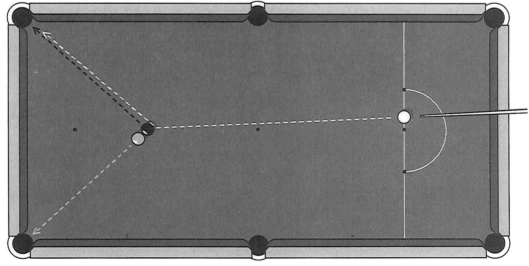

Part 2

TRICKIER
TRICK SHOTS

"Time to get tricky and impressive..."

33 LEAPING AHEAD OF THE PACK

Play this correctly and you'll believe a ball can fly! Put a triangle of reds to one side of the table, between the black and pink spots. Further down, stand the triangle on its base, facing the bottom left corner, and have the black over the pocket.

Strike down on the cue ball to leap over the pack. It will roll along, hit the triangle, jump through and pot the black.

You have to get a fair amount of height but don't overdo it. And don't forget to use that spare piece of baize to protect the table.

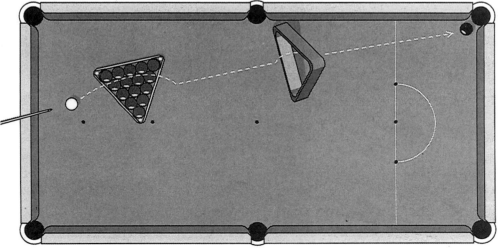

LAST JUMP TO FREEDOM 34

This looks spectacular but if you hit it right it shouldn't be difficult.

Black and red are tight against the cushion, by the baulk line, touching each other. Another two reds snuggle up at an angle. Stand the triangle on its base across the top left corner pocket and put four or five reds along it (one will have to just forward slightly from the rest because there won't be enough room to accommodate them all in a straight line.)

Strike the cue ball at six o'clock, with pace, to hit the nearest red, full in the face. The black will come out, run diagonally up the table, hit the triangle, jump over the reds and go into the corner pocket.

"A Big Break contestant had a go at this and broke the triangle. It was hastily repaired and i tried but the black kept missing the pocket. I had nine attempts before I realised that the triangle hadn't been stuck together properly! A replacement was found and the contestant then did it straight off. Jim Davidson announced, 'John Virgo 9, contestant 1!'"

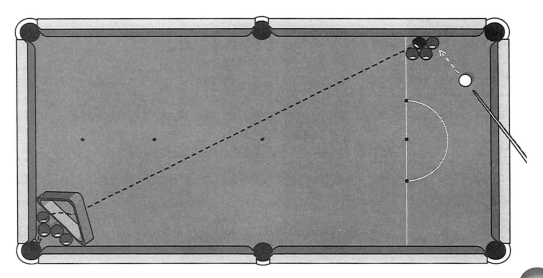

35 THE DOUBLE KISS DOUBLE

The black is tight against the left cushion and the white is in the middle of the table.

Strike the cue ball to hit the black just slightly to the right of full in the face and there will be a quick, double kiss as the black sinks into the cushion, springs back to clip off the white and crosses into the opposite pocket.

"There's no truth in the rumour that I learned the Double Kiss Double from Graham Miles when I shared a double bed with him in Ottawa! That's a viscious lie. We just slept together, that's all. I think I'd better explain . . .

These days when pros go overseas to play in tournaments they stay in big hotels and are only there for a day or two. But in 1972 Willie Thorne and myself where the only two amateurs to accompany the pros to Canada. The two big names on the circuit were Alex Higgins and Graham Miles and we stayed in a small log cabin where Graham and I had to share the same bed! I didn't mind though because I was in bed with the world number two!"

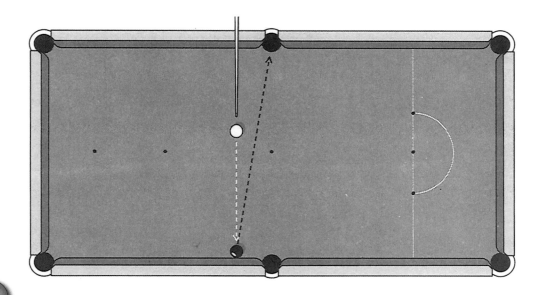

LOVER'S TIFF 36

This is an interesting shot. The black is tight against the cushion in front of the baulk line, and a red ball touches it. With the white positioned as shown, pot the black without moving the red.

Hit the cue ball at six o'clock – the harder the better – and the black will pot into the top right corner pocket whilst the red stays absolutely still.

I call it the Lover's Tiff because one moment they are touching, the next one of them storms off in a huff!

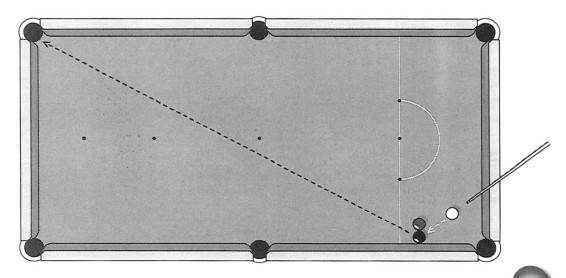

37 BLACK BALL SANDWICH

With the black ball sandwiched between the white and pink in line with the top right corner pocket, it looks impossible to pot.

However, by playing the white at two o'clock, using the loop bridge to aid follow, black pushes the pink out of the way as it makes its progress into the pocket.

Not another impression of Dennis Taylor!

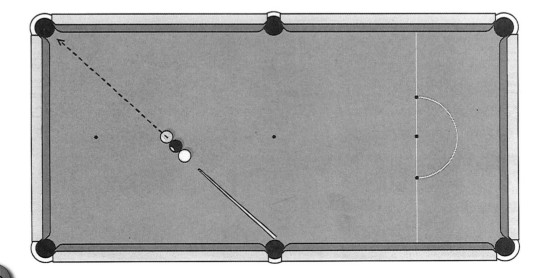

MAGNETIC ATTRACTION 38

The pink and the black are placed along the cushion with a red ball touching each, at an angle. With the cue ball positioned, as shown, state that you are going to pot the pink and black.

Strike the white at six o'clock, using the loop bridge, to hit the red. The pink springs across the table to pot centre left. The red carries on to hit the second red ball, which sends the black flying across the table to sink into the same pocket.

Karen Corr, Stacey Hillyard and Alison Fisher were some of the best lady snooker players in the world. All three of them were unable to make much of a living in the United Kingdom and went to ply their wares on the pool circuit in the USA. Karen and Alison really made their mark and have made a big name for themselves in America.

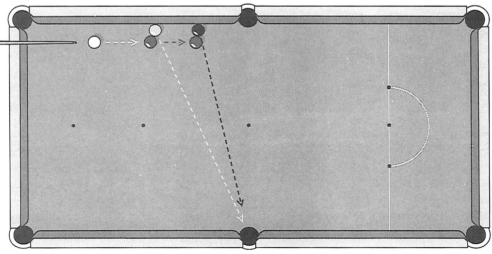

③⑨ PATHFINDER

As a variation to Shot 38, have a red ball as an obstacle in the black's path to the pocket. And this time you are just going to pot the black ball.

Strike the white as before. And the pink knocks the red away so that the black can pot.

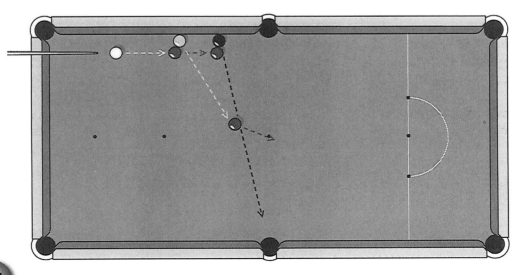

FORCING AN ENTRY 40

Two reds are side by side in the corner pocket with the black behind. Tell your friends that you will pot the black in the same pocket.

This shot is difficult with a cue, so don't use one!

Instead, hit the top of the black with your hand into the pocket. It will press into the reds, receive back-spin and come out, along with the reds. The black then reverses back through the gap into the pocket.

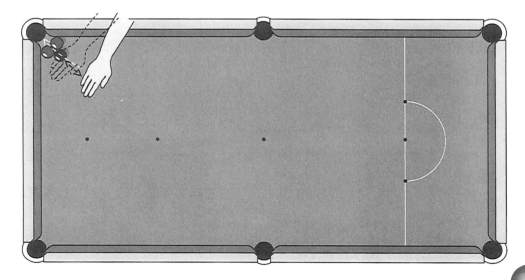

41 THE RUNWAY

There are several variations to this one. Put two cues together in line with the middle pocket, and a third fanning out. The black ball is over the middle pocket.

It's all about sending the ball around the angles again and judging the pace. The cue ball hits three sides, goes up the big gap in the cues, hops over and runs down the runway to hit the black into the pocket.

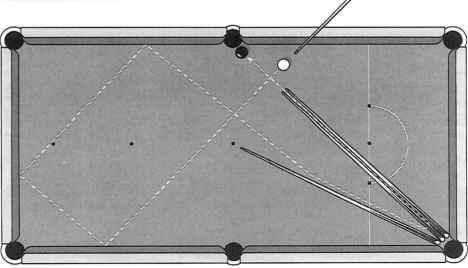

BLOCKED RUNWAY

You can make Shot 41 more difficult by holding a black ball on the end of the runway with a little piece of folded up paper. Then when the cue ball goes round the cushions and down the cues, it will hit the black which will down into the pocket.

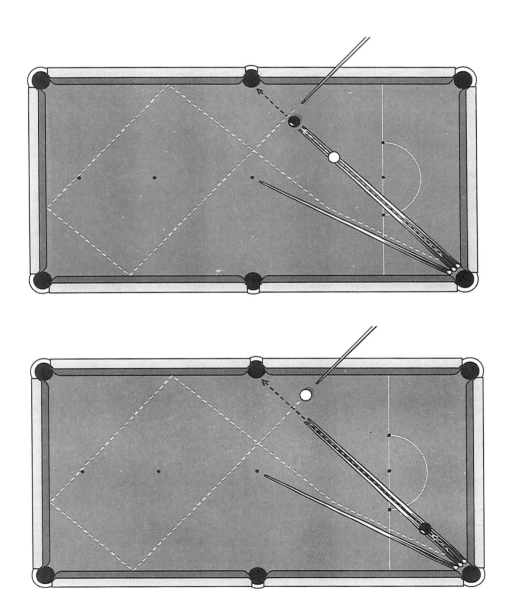

43 SENDING THE TROOPS IN

Yet more advanced! Leave the black on the cues and place a red over the middle pocket. As the white rolls down the cues, it knocks the black, which pots the red and, with a bit of luck, the white will catch up and knock the black in.

The beauty of this is that it's a good one to practice and will look great. You might find it better to place the black higher up the cues, towards the grips, depending on the speed of your table.

"When I first started doing my impressions on television, players such as Ray Reardon, would come up to me and ask why I wasn't doing them!

Alex Higgins is the only one who has taken offence. He injured his leg at one time and I did an impression of him, at Crucible Theatre, hopping around the table. But Alex didn't think it was at all amusing and he threatened to sue me! Then I explained to him: 'Look Alex, we're all in the business of entertaining people and you're the greatest entertainer of them all. It's just a bit of fun.' He pulled his face a bit, but took it on the chin."

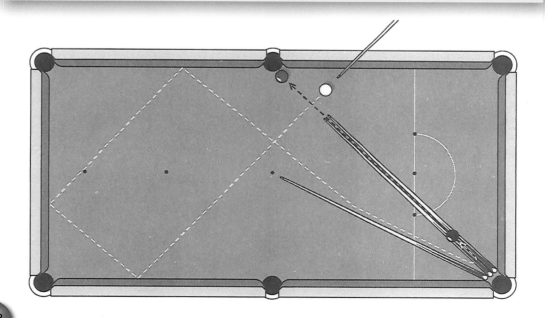

RAPID FIRE SHOT 44

Show off with flair and maximum noise with this shot that looks – and sounds – impressive but is not difficult if you hit the balls properly at the correct part of the cushion.

Two cues fan out from the top corner pocket and another two cues lie flush against both cushions. Take five or more balls and line them up by the right middle pocket. Then send them round three cushions, hitting them rapidly, one after the other. And they run up the cues, chasing each other, clattering into the corner pocket.

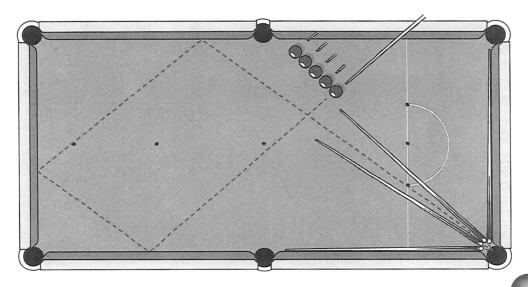

45 FINE CUT

In contrast to the last few shots, there are no gimmicks here. It's just a very fine shot.

Put the black ball on its spot and from the yellow spot, pot the black into the top right corner pocket. It doesn't look possible but it will go if you make very thin contact with the black.

The basket has been used in trick shots for donkey's years. It's a great prop. The one I used on *Big Break* was provided by the BBC, but unfortunately I know of nowhere that you can buy them. The only thing I can do here is to give you the dimensions and if you know of someone who is a dab hand at wicker work, they will be able to make one for you!

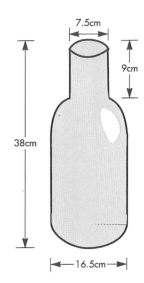

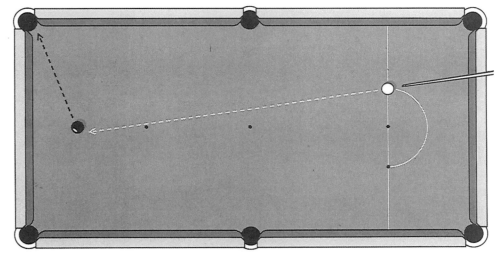

BASKET FLIP 46

A simple one to begin with where the basket is placed on its neck on the blue spot. The black is over the middle pocket and the white in a line over the other side.

The idea is to pot the black and turn the basket the right way up at the same time. All you need to do is to judge how hard to strike the cue ball.

The man on the right is Bryan Blackburn – a very funny man and scriptwriter. He also wrote the hit song 'Welcome Home' sung by Peters and Lee.

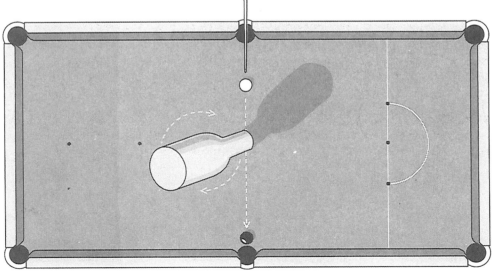

47 HOLE IN ONE

Here the basket is again standing on its neck, with the black ball placed on top. Strike the cue ball very hard, just above centre, to hit the basket and turn it over. The black should then pot middle right.

"I haven't been able to do any impressions of the newer generation of snooker players because they grew up watching Steve Davis on television in the Eighties when he was outstandingly successful and naturally modelled themselves on him. Unfortunately for me, Steve doesn't have any mannerisms and rarely shows any emotion. But Stephen Hendry has one or two peculiarities so I might start working on him!"

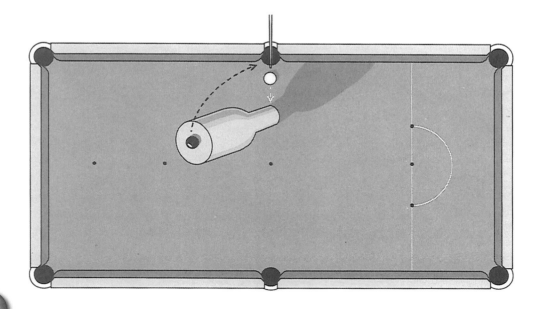

DOWN THE TUBE 48

Now for the tube shot. Place the tallest tube near the middle pocket with a red ball on top of it. The black is over the pocket on the other side. Hit the white into the tube and the red rolls across the table and pots the black.

You'll need a few goes at it in order to judge the optimum position for the tube. We'll come back to the tubes later for some more difficult shots.

The tube is another prop of the trick shot specialist. It must be about a ball and a half tall, just high enough to allow a ball to go underneath. Mine is made of a light wood and provided by the BBC. But you can make your own from a Smartie tube strengthened with stiff cardboard or papier-mâché. Make two whilst you're at it, because you will also need a taller version two and a half balls high.

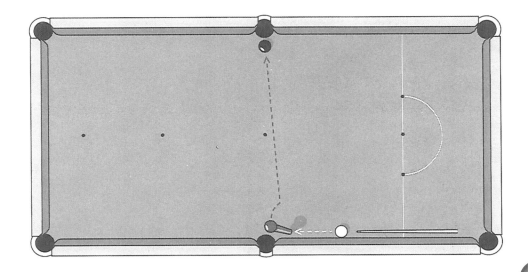

49 SLIDE BALL

The black ball is over the bottom left pocket and the cue ball tight on the right hand cushion. Slide the white up the cushion with the middle of the cue and the side imparted on the ball causes it to rebound off the top cushion diagonally across the table to pot the black.

This next one doesn't always work but it does sometimes and I'm not sure why! I played it successfully on *Big Break*, so good luck and let me know how you get on!

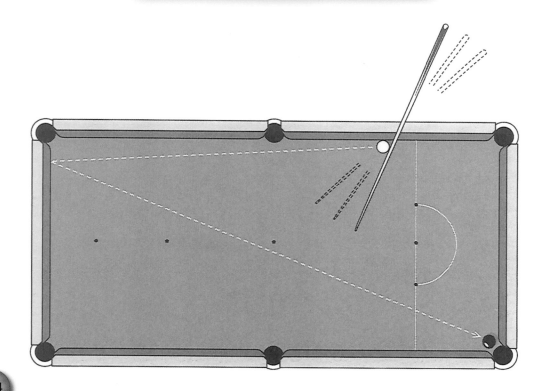

SLIDE BALL PART TWO 50

A variation of Slide Ball with two balls. The black stays where it was before and the pink is positioned over the top right pocket. And in front of the white ball, place a red. The trick is to pot both the pink and black in one shot.

Slide the white and red down the table with the action you used before, and the red will pot the pink whilst the white rebounds off the top cushion to pot the black.

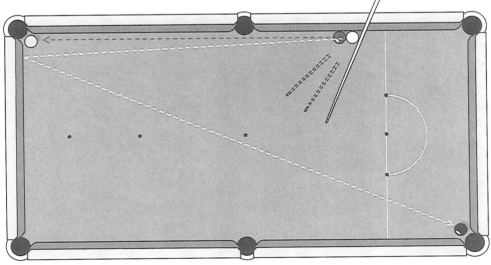

51 CHOPSTICKS

Pick a ball up with two cues chopsticks style. Hold the cues together with one hand at the back and in the middle with the other hand as if you are holding chopsticks. Squeeze the ball against the side of the cushion so that it will roll onto the cues. Lift them off the table and drop the ball into a pocket of your choice!

If you find it too difficult, you can always ask for a knife and fork (only kidding!)

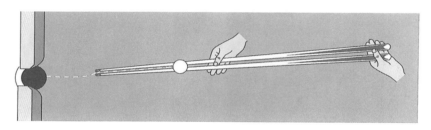

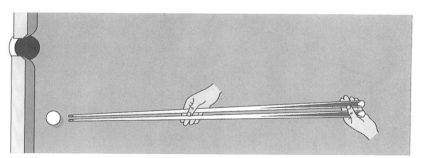

ROLLERBALL

Hold your two cues together with one hand and place one ball on top of another with your other hand.

Place your cues on top of the balls and by tilting the cues you can move the balls around and pot them in any pocket.

"Jim Davidson is great to work with. We have so much fun that after we finish filming a series I get withdrawal symptoms and can't wait to start work on the next one. He takes the mickey out of me a lot on the show but because we got on so well together I don't mind."

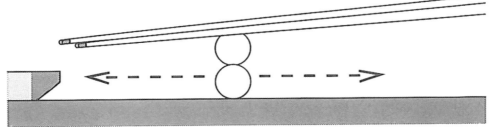

For the last two years I have been touring with the 'Snooker Legends'. I open with trick shots which I set up for a member of the audience to do.

We have great fun on the tour, particularly with the likes of Jimmy White, John Parrot, Dennis Taylor and Cliff Thorburn.

Last year in Dundalk we had a raffle to give someone a chance to play a frame with Jimmy White and win a cue. The lucky ticket holder came down to the table and said, firstly, that he had his own cue and, secondly, that he wanted to be announced as 'Tornado' Terry. So that's what I did, "Jimmy 'Whirlwind' White will play 'Tornado' Terry".

While the 'Tornado' was putting his cue together, the 'Whirlwind' broke off, hit the reds from behind and fluked one in the middle pocket. He then proceeded to clear the fifteen reds and blacks to make a 147.

'Tornado' Terry didn't even have to chalk his cue! We will never know how good he was....

THE DOUBLE HIT SHOT 53

A gentle and accurate touch is required here. The black ball is over the bottom right pocket and the white is behind the baulk line.

Strike the white at six o'clock which will send it forward and, if you really catch it right, it should come back strongly off the top cushion. As it does so, check it at six o'clock again with your cue. It will hop forward and swerve onto the black to make the pot.

That's the last time I have my hair permed. It makes me look like Terry Griffiths!

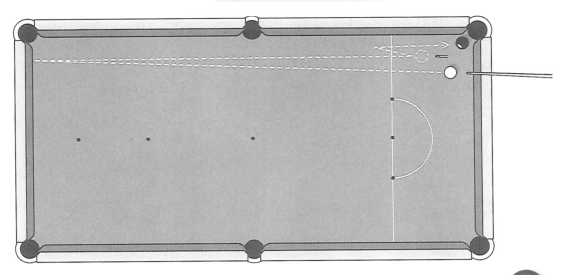

54 TUBEE OR NOT TUBEE

Place the black ball on the tallest tube over the middle pocket and the pink in the middle of the table. Strike the cue ball in the middle. It hits the pink, which knocks away the tube and pots. The white follows and pots the black.

Pot the pink...

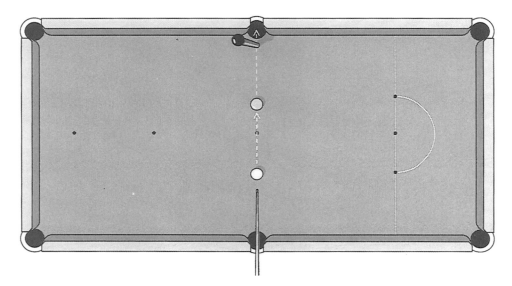

... and then the black

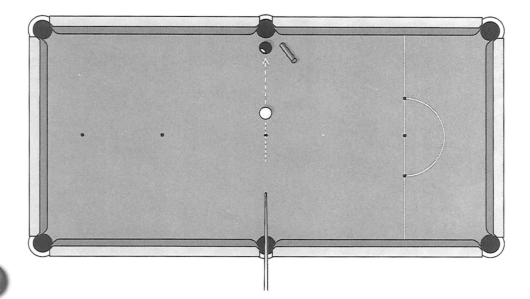

FLYING PINK

If you really want to be adventurous . . . put the black on the tube again. The white tight against the opposite side and the pink above it, perched on top of the cushion.

Strike the pink to run across the table, and knock the tube away as it pots. The black drops and the pink will have sent the white moving by rolling across the top of it. White then pots the black.

Pink flies across ...

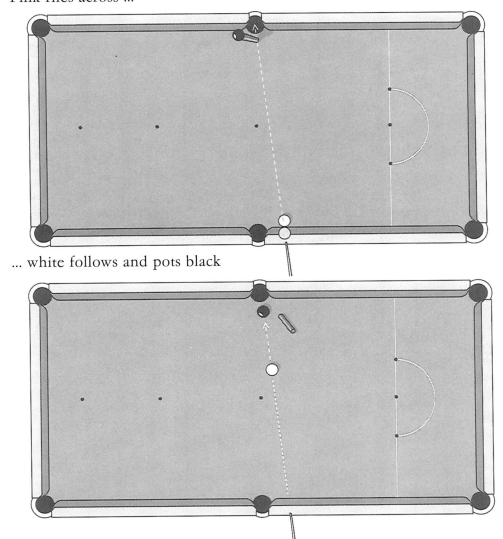

... white follows and pots black

56 DISAPPEARING REDS

Have two reds touching in the middle of the table and the line of aim is the near edge of the corner pockets on the left side (as marked). This is because you need to play a push shot which will send the two reds forward a touch before they travel outwards. Place another red in front. Now you are going to pot all three balls in three pockets.

Use the loop bridge because there is resistance against a cue ball when it's touching another ball so you need to keep the cue down to get it through smoothly.

Strike the cue ball at twelve o'clock, pushing through with pace to give it the thrust to get through the reds. And they pot middle and corner pockets.

"I liven up my trick shot section on Big Break by wearing outrageous waistcoats. The more garish the better, as far as I'm concerned. The first time I came on wearing one Jim said I was wearing a 'No dad'. I'd never heard the expression before so I asked what it meant and he said it was when kids had to wear clothes they hated and would moan, 'Oh, no dad, don't make me wear that!'"

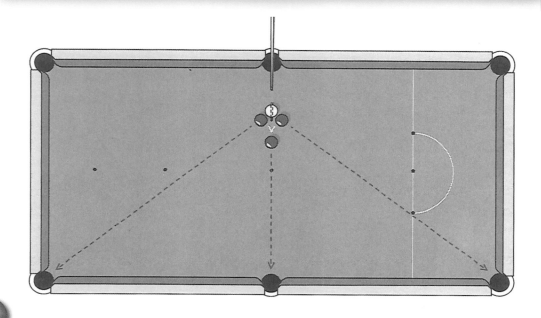

DISAPPEARING REDS – THE SEQUEL 57

A variation is to have a red over the top right corner pocket and the white touching two reds lined up with the top left corner pocket and right middle.

Play the shot in the same way as before to pot three balls in three pockets.

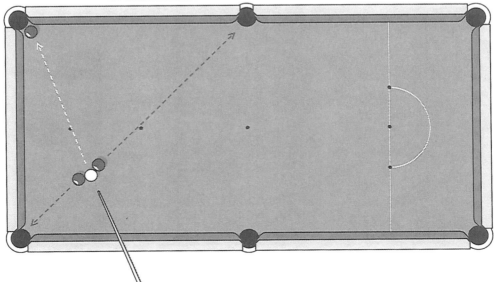

58 BANANA SHOT

This is a very handy shot to know where you are playing snooker. A red ball is over the top left corner pocket and the black nearer in from the top cushion. The aim is to pot the red and get position on the black.

Strike the cue ball from behind the baulk line with extreme top and it pots the red and curves around the black to where it is in a good position to pot the black with your next shot to win a frame.

"A lady called Jane Rolfe makes the waistcoats I wear on Big Break and I have a different one for every programme. I particularly like my Batman and Bart Simpson ones.

People expect me to wear them wherever I go now, so I always put one on for exhibitions and after dinner events.

But I can be on a golf course or a beach in my swimming trunks and someone will say 'I see you've not got your waistcoat on today!'"

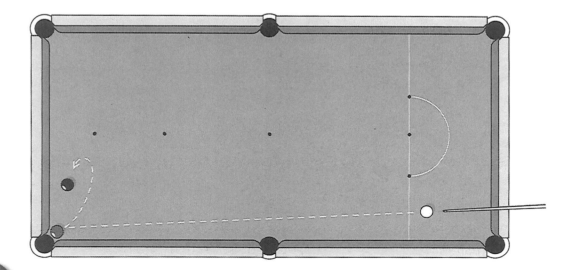

59 GRAND CANYON

It's basket time again. This shot is the same principle as jumping over the triangle. Lie the basket on its side with the white in front. And you strike down on the ball for it to jump into the neck of the basket.

If you fancy yourself as a motorbike stunt rider. You can put a line of balls between the basket and the white so that you can see how far you can get a ball to jump on target. Gradually increase the number each time until you have six or more.

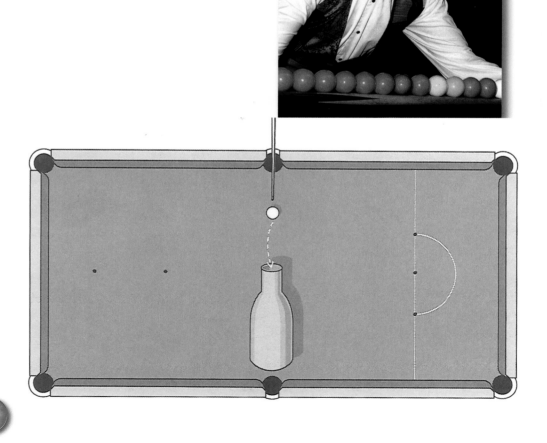

MAGIC COLOUR

Secretly put a red ball inside the basket, just below the neck and lie it on the table. Now announce that you are going to hit the white ball into the basket and it will come out red.

Hit the cue ball in from an angle. The basket will spin and the red pops out.

When I did this on *Big Break* the red flew into the pocket and everyone said, 'tremendous'. But it was only luck. You're not expected to pot anything with this shot, but I kept quiet about it being a fluke!

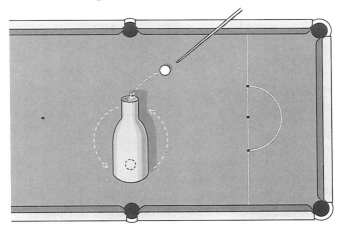

Even Paul Daniels can't do this.

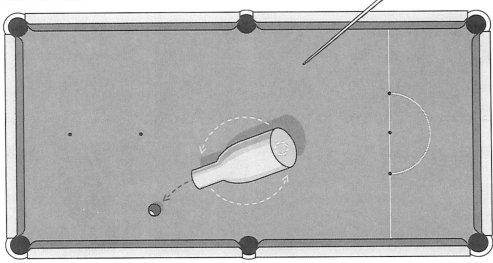

61 FROZEN WHITE

Place the black over the bottom right pocket, the pink over the top left and the white sandwiched between two reds tight on the top cushion. Pot the pink and black without moving the white.

Play a red cue ball from the brown spot, hitting it hard to make thin contact on the end red, and it deflects into the pocket. The second red is sent up the table to pot the black and the third red runs across the cushion to pot the pink. The white remains frozen.

"John Spencer's success inspired me when I was making my way up as an amateur. We were from the same area - he's from Bolton and I'm from Salford – and we would read in snooker magazines about events and players in London and felt a bit like we were being treated second class because we lived in the north. Then, all of a sudden, Spencer won the English Amateur Championship, turned professional and became World Champion a couple of years later. I think everyone's game, in our area, improved by about twenty points because we could relate to Spencer and now knew the level we had to reach."

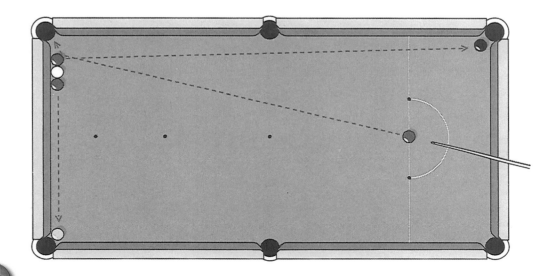

The great Houdini would be proud of the escape the black ball does here from the clutches of the reds.

Place the black on the pink spot, surrounded by six reds, touching each other and the black except at the ends.

Strike the cue ball at six o'clock to hit the first red full in the face. It makes simultaneous contact with second red and the black. The third red is cleared away and the black makes a half-ball contact with the fourth red and pots middle left.

The tube shot Marion Ramsey of Police Academy did this one from my trickshot videos.

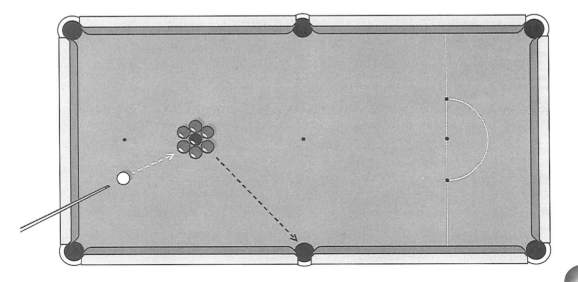

TUBULAR BALLS

Take both of your tubes, position the tallest on the blue spot and put the black ball on top. The smaller tube goes next to it with the pink ball on top, almost touching the big tube.

Strike the cue ball to knock the tubes away, the balls drop to the table, make a half-ball contact and knock each other in opposite directions. Black goes into the middle right pocket and pink into the middle left.

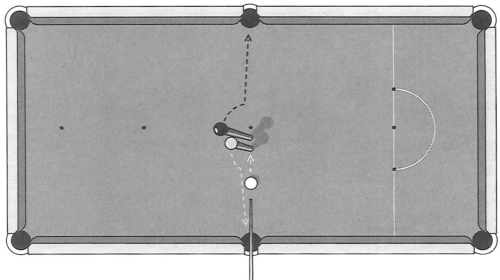

64 CONFUSION SOLUTION

Set the reds up with the triangle. Then put the black slightly out of line as shown, a red further away from the pack and two other touching reds opposite. Pot the black in the top right pocket.

As you can see, the two stray reds are in the way so you play a cannon. Strike the cue ball at twelve o'clock, hitting the first red on the side. This red rolls across to knock the other two balls out of the way. The white cannons into the reds sending the black into the pocket.

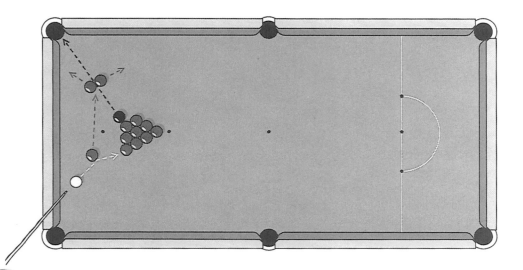

INTERCEPTOR 65

This is a good shot. Put the black and white, touching, against the left cushion, about four balls away from the pocket. And from there you are going to pot the black in the middle left pocket.

Hit the white across the table, the black moves along the cushion and the white pots in on the rebound.

The harder you hit this one, the easier it is and the better it will look. The point to aim for is the near corner of the middle pocket. You won't be able to hit this mark though, because the black pushes the white off.

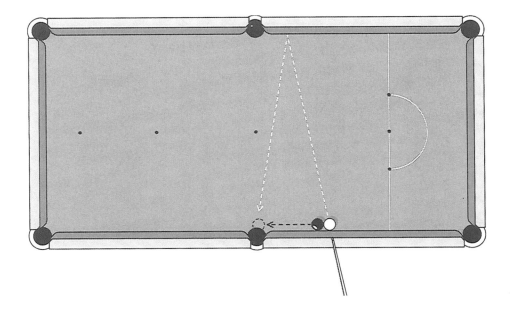

66 DISAPPEARING REDS THE THIRD

This is a more elaborate version of Shot 57. Two red balls touch each other at an angle up the table. Towards the other end another couple of reds touch the white ball.

All four reds are going to be potted in four pockets. Again, it's a push shot so position the balls in line with the near edges of the pockets as indicated.

Push the cue ball through the first two reds, using the loop bridge, sending them into the side pockets. The white travels onto the other two reds, potting them into the corner pockets. It's a difficult shot and I wish you the best of luck!

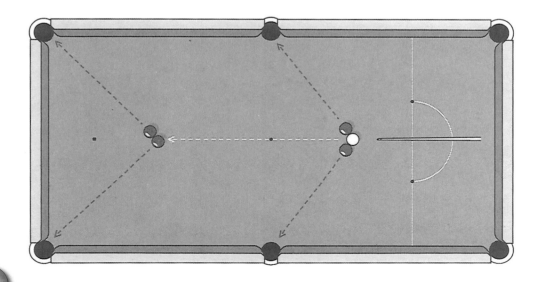

Part 3

T RY 'EM

IF YOU DARE

"Pull these off and you're a legend..."

67 GOING GOING GONE

The black is over the bottom right pocket and two reds are tight on the right cushion, about half an inch apart.

Hit the cue ball hard, at one o'clock, in the middle of the reds. They move away and the white pots the black.

Generally speaking the more balls you have on the table the better the shot will look because the surprise will be which one you are going to pot. And then your audience will wonder how on earth you are going to get past all the other balls.

Keep 'em guessing as you set up your shots. Then, when you are ready, say what you are going to do and then promptly do it.

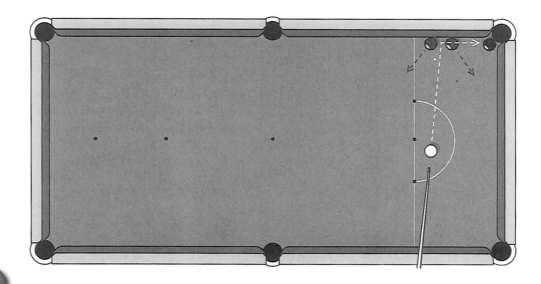

STRAIGHT DOWN THE MIDDLE 68

This is a tough shot but you have entered Try 'Em If You Dare territory! Two rows of five reds, almost touching, are aligned slightly off the middle right pocket, just in front of the blue spot. Another two reds and the black are behind, all touching. And the idea is to pot the black in the middle pocket.

I suggest playing the cue ball at eight o'clock to hit the first red on the left side, which will spin it over to the black. In other words, it's a plant on the second red and black.

Because it slightly moves the second red first, the top line will move quicker. Both lines rub off each other and the reds disperse outwards. The black then runs down the middle into the pocket. It might not look like it will, but that's the beauty of the shot!

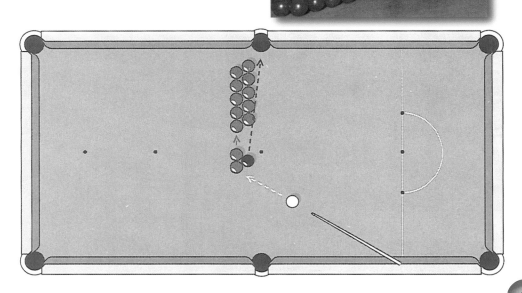

69 TUBE-TASTIC

Place the black on the tube against the side cushion just in front of the middle right pocket. The white is also against the cushion with a red ball in between. Two more reds are positioned to the left of the tube. Pot the black in the middle left pocket.

The reds are in the way of the shot so a cannon is required. The cue ball is tight on the cushion so you have to strike it slightly above centre. Hit the first red on the right side, playing a cannon onto the other reds to disperse them.

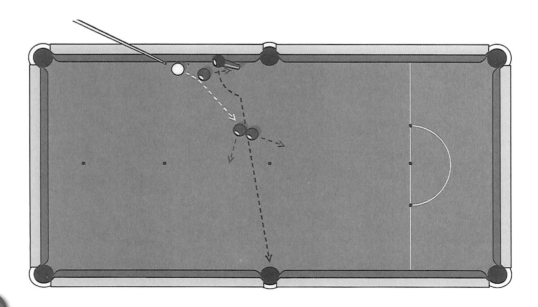

With this shot we're going one step further from bouncing the ball through the triangle. Don't forget the spare piece of baize to protect the table!

The black is over the corner pocket, the white ball to its right and the red forming a triangle. Announce that you will pot the white in that pocket, off the red. Everyone can see that the black ball is in the way so they will wonder how it's done. Strike down on the cue ball and it will jump up and go in off the red, leap-frogging the black.

Alex Higgins became my second big inspiration, after John Spencer. I used to love watching him play and I realised that the game didn't have to be slow and boring. I started to have fun in my snooker club doing an impression of him.

"I always remember going into the snooker club in South Wales, when Higgins was at his height. He'd just won the world championship and had been playing exhibitions everywhere. People were amazed at the speed and talent of the man. There were ten tables in this club and everyone was trying to play like Higgins, running around the tables, bumping into each other. It was an exciting time because he showed how the game could be played and spawned many imitators."

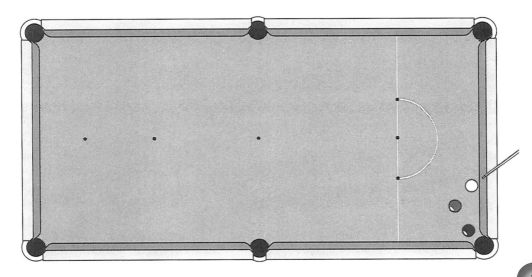

71 THE M-25 SHOT

This one looks pretty spectacular. It will take a while to set up so you'll have to study the diagram for a few hours! The pairs of reds are all touching and the bottom two also touch the pink and black. A solitary red is placed by the middle right pocket and this is where you are going to pot the black. Ready? Take a deep breath and have a go.

Strike the cue ball at seven o'clock, with some pressure, to hit the first red full in the face.

It moves the inner red away and goes on to hit the second outer red. That does the same, and so on. The third outer red plays a plant on the three balls, sending the pink off the bottom cushion which plays a plant in turn so that the black runs up the cushion and is nudged into the middle pocket by the final red. Phew!

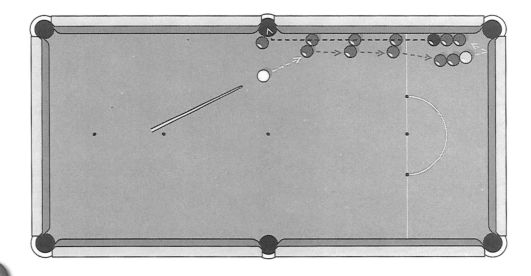

REDS IN THEIR BEDS

Remember what I said about the nap of the baize being brushed towards the black spot? Well, set this one up at the top of the table because you'll need the black to hug the cushion.

Three reds are placed near the pink spot, two of them touching. And a trail of reds are along the cushion with the black on the end of the middle group. A solitary red stands in the way of its route into the top left pocket.

Strike the cue ball hard at six o'clock to hit the first red full in the face. Red 2 cannons red 3 out of the way. The plant on red 4 sends it across the table, where it bounces off the side cushion and hits the trail of reds.

The end ball hits the next cluster, causing the black to break away and roll towards the pocket. You can have a red by the pocket to make it easier, in case the black needs a nudge in, but it shouldn't be necessary.

Once again the element of surprise makes this a spectacular shot. The more balls you set up with this the better.

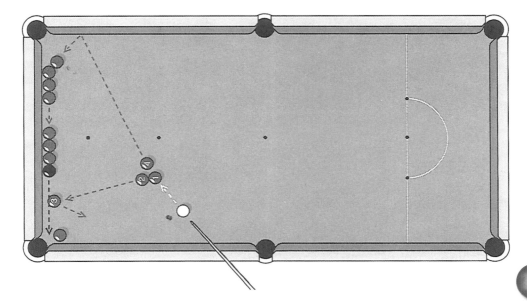

73 THE HURDLE SHOT

Place the rest across the table with the X on the top of the side cushion as shown, and a red ball underneath. The white is in front and the black is over the corner pocket. Tell everyone that you are going to jump the white over the rest and it will come back under to pot the black. Try to convince yourself too!

Strike down on the cue ball, hitting it on the bottom to get the back-spin required. It hits the red, jumps the rest and back-spins under the rest to pot the black.

It's a difficult shot and I decided to do it one night at an exhibition. I gave it a big build up, did it first time and everyone gave a look as if to say, 'Is that it? We want more than that!'

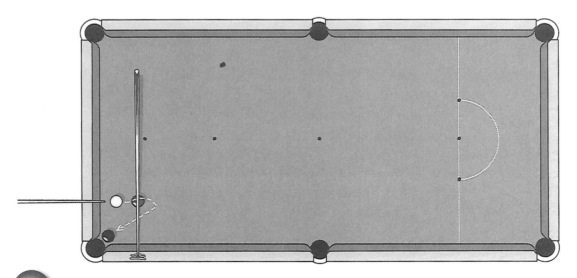

74 DEATHSLIDE

Another variation of the cue shots we did earlier. Two cues by the corner pocket again, pointing towards the middle pocket, and a third fanned out. The pink is over the top right pocket, the blue and red touching in line with the middle right pocket, the black to one side and the white against the cushion. Pot the blue, pink and black in order.

Strike the cue ball at three o'clock. It makes thin contact with the red which knocks the blue in on its way to potting the pink. The white goes around the angles, up the gap in the cues, jumps over and down to pot the black.

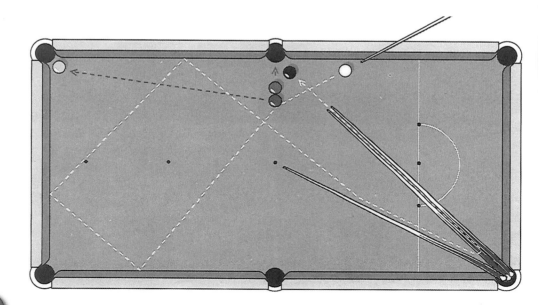

RETURN OF THE TUBE 75

This is one I dazzled them with at the World Trick Shot Championship.

Again, it's potting the blue, pink and black with one shot, but this time all in the same pocket. The blue is on its spot, the pink just to one side of the middle right pocket, and the black on the tube in front of it.

Strike the cue ball at three o'clock to catch the left hand side of the blue so that it pots centre right. The white rebounds off the top cushion, hits the tube and goes through to pot the pink. The black falls off the tube and runs across the table to the opposite middle pocket.

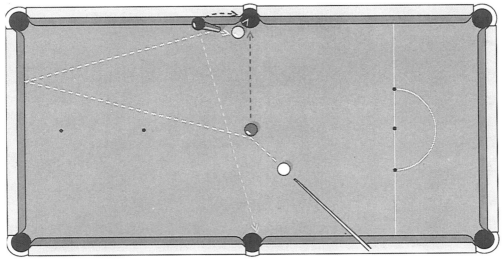

76 CHASE THE BLACK

The black is just by the baulk line and the white behind it. Send the black around the table and, immediately after hitting it, play the white in the same way, but harder, so that it chases the black around the table.

If you get the pace and the angle right, the white will gain on the black and help it into the bottom left pocket just before it drops.

"I modelled myself first on Spencer then on Higgins as I was making my way up in the game of snooker. I'm not as fast as Higgins but I've never been a slow player. The thing with Higgins is that he has this small, darting appearance where everything seems to be happening at great speed – even when he's lighting his cigarette! I've got a different stature, and so has Willie Thorne. But I always thought that Willie was a much quicker player than Alex."

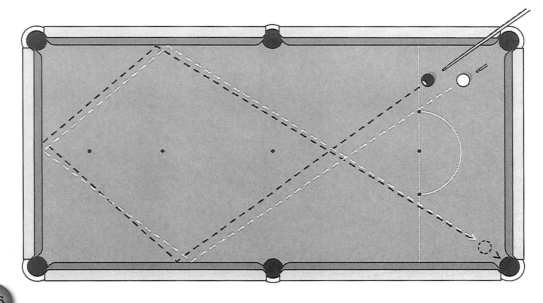

MOVING TARGETS

A variation of the last Shot 76 is to play the black in the same way. Wait until it comes off the final cushion then pot it in the middle left pocket with the cue ball.

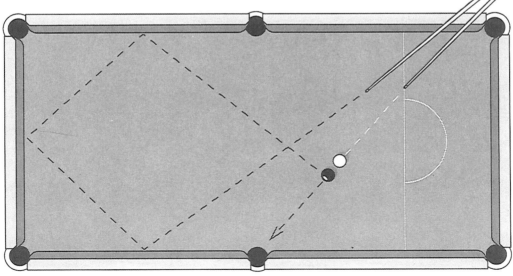

78 BIRD IN THE HAND

The success rate with this isn't too high, I have to warn you! Have two reds near the pink spot with the black and the pink touching them at an angle in line with the top left and middle left pockets. The gap between the two reds is not wide enough for a ball to go between.

They are set up for a plant. The idea is to jump the white over the reds, bounce off the side cushion, come back, hit the two reds and knock the pink and black in. It can be done, like all the shots in this book. Good luck!

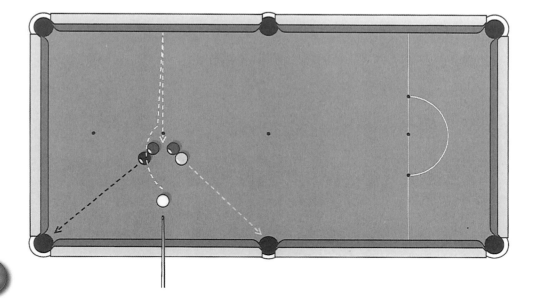

Eddie Kid taught me this shot – only he did it on a motorbike!

Six reds are spaced out from the baulk line. And the pink and black are further up the table lined up to go into the top corner pockets.

Strike down on the cue ball to fly over the reds and hit the black full in the face to send the balls into the pockets.

Once you've mastered it, place a glass of wine or bottle of milk behind the pink and black, just to scare whoever owns the table.

Sometimes snooker trick shots can get a bit ambitious. So I always warn the Big Break crew to stand well back!

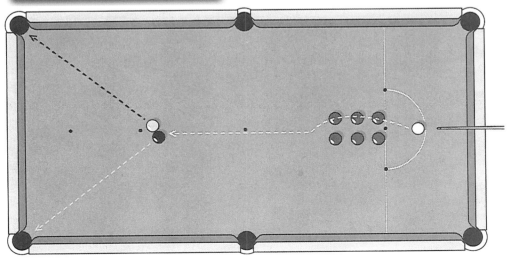

80 OVERGROUND, UNDERGROUND

A new prop this time – the spider rest – for elevation. Place it across the table with the spider on the wood of the cushion. Put the black over the bottom right pocket and the pink near the middle left pocket.

Strike down on the cue ball at ten o'clock for it to jump and get left side-spin at the same time. It hits the pink on the right side which rolls under the cue and pots in the middle pocket. The white jumps the spider, and bounces off three cushions to pot the black.

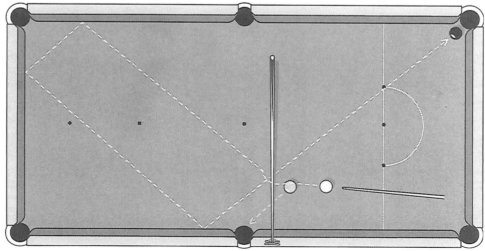

MACHINE GUN SHOT

A line of six reds and the white face the corner pocket. Slowly roll the white towards the pocket, and before it reaches there, you pot the six reds so that the white is the last to drop.

I saw Tony Knowles try this with fifteen balls for a record. Unfortunately, it's hard for the pocket to take that many balls, but the more you do, the more impressive it is.

"I've always greatly admired Ray Reardon. I won a lot of amateur tournaments and became established as one of the best in the world, but I will never forget the comeuppance I received at the hands of Ray in 1975. They used to have a Pontins Holiday Camp Pro/Am tournament. I went there as an amateur and the professional had to give you a twenty five point start, when really the top amateurs thought they were as good as them. I got to the final without too much trouble where I met Reardon, who was the World Champion, and he murdered me! It wasn't that I was complacent I just felt insulted to be given a lead and I honestly believe, to this day, that if I'd played him level, it would have been a closer match."

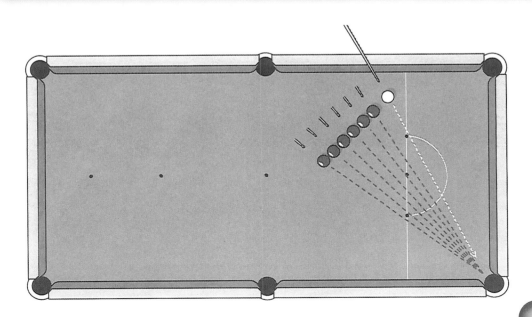

82 PRO'S PARTY PIECE

Here's a party piece that all the pros seem to be playing these days. Pot the black off four cushions. Place the black on its spot and hit the cue ball hard at five o'clock. And it pots in the top right pocket.

I used to fill in for Ray Reardon for exhibitions at holiday camps. He is such a good character that we always had a great laugh whenever we met up.

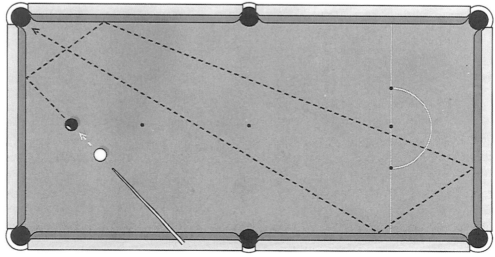

SIX CUSHION BONANZA 83

If you had fun with the last shot, try this one to pot the black off six cushions! But this time we place the black to one side of the bottom left pocket and play the cue ball from the black spot. As it bounces off a cushion for the final time, it clips the black into the pocket.

"It was whilst I was in Ottawa that I first realised my potential for comedy. As I've mentioned, I'd already seen Jackie Rea perform, but being an amateur I didn't play many exhibitions. It was all very intense because I was trying to prove myself to people.

I was asked to open the balls up for Graham Miles so that he could show off his potting skill in an exhibition. I didn't have my own cue with me so I borrowed one and, because it was a bit sticky, I started to clean it with my tie. Suddenly, everybody fell about laughing. The tour organiser later told me that I would have to include it in an act because the look on my face had been hilarious. But I was being serious!"

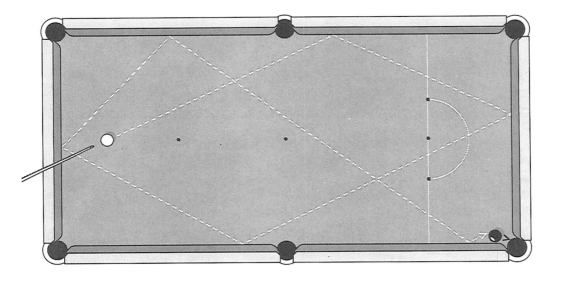

If someone had asked me before 'Big Break' how many trick shots I had in my repertoire the reply would have been about 15 maximum. But, as they say – needs must – because in the end we made nearly two hundred shows. I am not suggesting that's how many tricks I performed, but it helped me put together the one hundred trick shots for this book.

I must mention the help that was given by most of the players who appeared on the show. In particular Ray Reardon who was always ready with a shot idea. Earlier I mentioned the holiday camp circuit. Later on in my career I had the pleasure of filling in for Ray three or four weeks during the summer at the Pontins Holiday camps in the south Devon area.

Filling in for Ray was the main reason I took up golf as Ray would do the exhibitions in the morning so he could play golf in the afternoon. Someone once asked Ray what he thought was the main difference between golf and snooker and he replied: "I have been playing snooker for fifty years and never lost a ball".

ANNIE OAKLEY 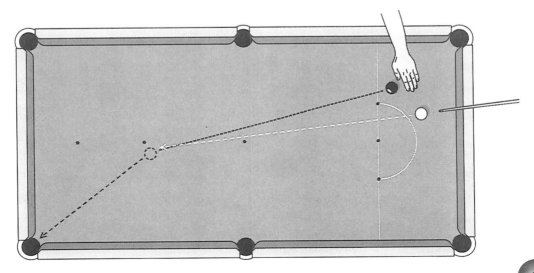84

I picked this one up when I was in the Wild West, where it pays to be quick on the draw. Pot the red whilst it's moving.

Roll the red up the table and pot with the cue ball in the top left pocket. It's a good exercise for 'getting your eye in' before a game.

Hopefully, with practice, you can become very good at one of the more difficult shots and it can be your party piece. You can then have the pleasure of telling other people how to do it.

85 FORE!

Ronnie O'Sullivan had ten attempts at this, so be patient!

Place the pink over the right middle pocket and three reds over the opposite pocket with the brown on the end, all touching. The blue should be over the top left pocket and the black over the bottom left corner.

Strike the cue ball to hit the middle two reds simultaneously. Ball 1 will knock the brown in centre left as it runs up the table and pots the blue. Ball 2 will have knocked ball 3 across the table to sink the pink. And as ball 2 travels up the table it will come back down to pot the black ... with a bit of luck and a following wind!

You could place the triangle on the table to channel the last red towards the black if it comes a bit wide.

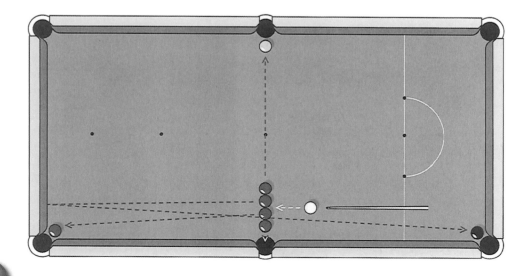

A more advanced version of Shot 85. This time, with just two red balls and the pink by the middle pocket. One of the reds is aimed towards the top corner and the green is placed over this pocket. The black and blue remain as before.

Strike the cue ball at six o'clock, hitting red 1 full in the face. It sinks the pink centre left as it runs up the table to pot the blue. Number 2 red travels diagonally across the table to pot the green and the white screws back down the table to pot the black.

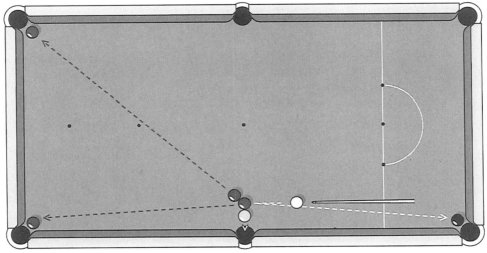

87 RUBY NECKLACE

A cluster of touching reds surrounds the corner pocket. A solitary red is to one side of the opening. The black is against the side cushion with the cue ball near to the top cushion. Pot the black. It looks impossible, but don't despair. This is a good one if you can pull it off.

Strike the cue ball to hit the black full in the face. It bounces off the cushion and travels around the reds into the pocket.

The most important thing is to get the cue ball to stop dead after it has hit the black so strike it in the middle, not too low – we don't want it to screw back and get in the way of the black running around the reds.

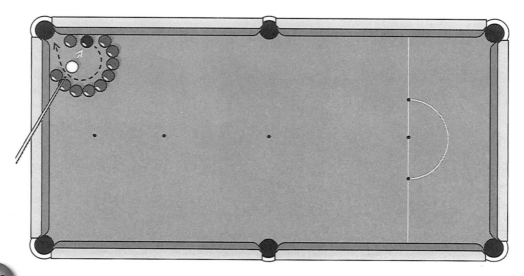

BACK OF THE NET

As a bit of fun. If you want to be really sneaky, put the black over the bottom left pocket. Leave the cue ball surrounded by the reds and say you're going to pot the black.

Then just put the cue through the netting of the pocket, hit the white up into the air to jump over the reds and pot the black.

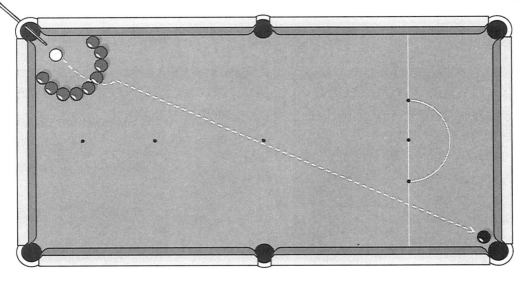

89 BREAKOUT

Yet another alternative. The black is now over the top left pocket and the cue ball positioned as before. Hit the cue ball against the right side cushion, striking slightly down, and it jumps over the reds and pots the black.

With all these shots it's not so much about managing to do some every now and then. It's the success rate which really matters.

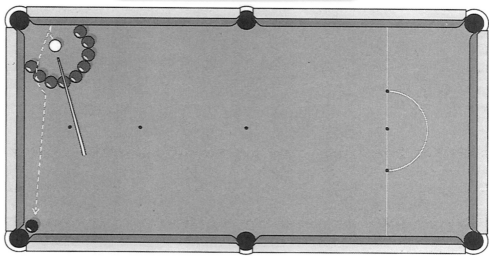

TAKE A REST 90

This takes a fair amount of accuracy in ball jumping. Lie the rest on top of the cushion, almost touching the black ball which is also on top, near the corner pocket. The white and red are nearby on the table. Now pot the black.

Strike down on the cue ball at six o'clock and it will jump off the red onto the side cushion, run down the rest and pot the black.

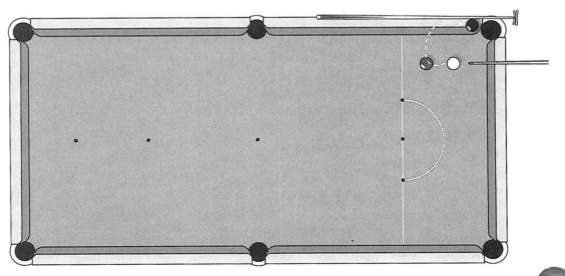

91 DISTANT COUSINS

Two red balls and the pink are touching on the left side cushion. And another red is by the centre pocket. The black is over the top left pocket. The aim is to pot the pink and black.

Strike the cue ball at seven o'clock to hit the left side of the end red and play a plant on the pink which runs along the cushion and pots on the centre pocket, off the red. The white rebounds off three cushions and pots the black.

92 BACK TO BLACK

Place the black to one side of the bottom left pocket and the pink on the other. To pot both colours, strike the cue ball at two o'clock, to clip the right side of the pink, and it will run into the pocket. The cue ball comes round three sides and knocks the black in.

"I mentioned earlier that patter is important when you are playing trick shots but I remember playing an exhibition in Belgium to an audience who couldn't really understand English, so most of my trick shots were done in silence!

Because I was thinking so much in visual terms, when it came to doing my impression of Alex Higgins, I got the idea to unscrew my two-piece cue in half and pretend there was a drink in the thicker end. I put it to my lips and it brought the house down."

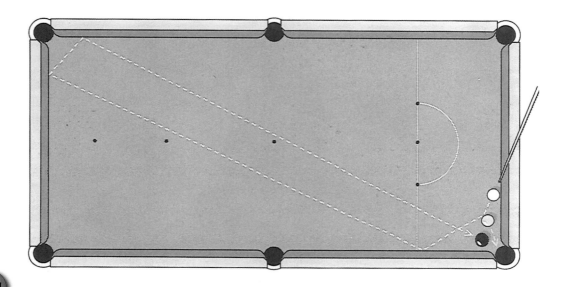

RED TRIANGLE 93

Fill the triangle with reds and place at an angle between the black and pink spots. The black is over the bottom left pocket and the pink is to the left of the triangle. Once again, pot both colours.

Strike the cue ball at five o'clock to hit the pink on the right side which will pot in the corner pocket. The white cannons onto the triangle where it rebounds onto the side cushion and runs down the table to pot the black.

These next few shots will really test your knowledge of the angles ...

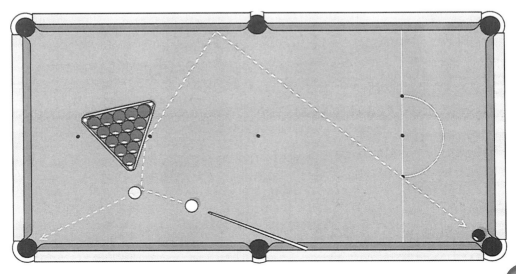

94 CLIP THE RED

This is a billiard shot which is difficult enough on its own but it's only a warm-up for Shot 96!

With the red and the black touching on the side cushion, strike the cue ball, with pace, at three o'clock to clip the right side of the red, thereby playing a plant which moves the black along the cushion.

The cue ball cannons off, hitting the side and bottom cushions before it makes contact with the moving black.

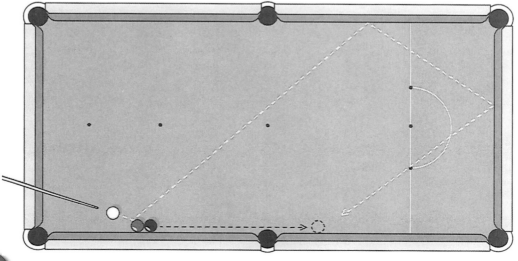

DOUBLE TROUBLE 95

This is a variation of Shot 94 with two reds and the black touching on the side cushion and the pink over the bottom of the left pocket.

Strike the cue ball at five o'clock, clipping the side of the red. The black runs up the cushion and pots the pink. The white then comes around the table, off three cushions, and pots the black.

A difficult shot but a good one to practice until you judge it just right.

Pot the pink ...

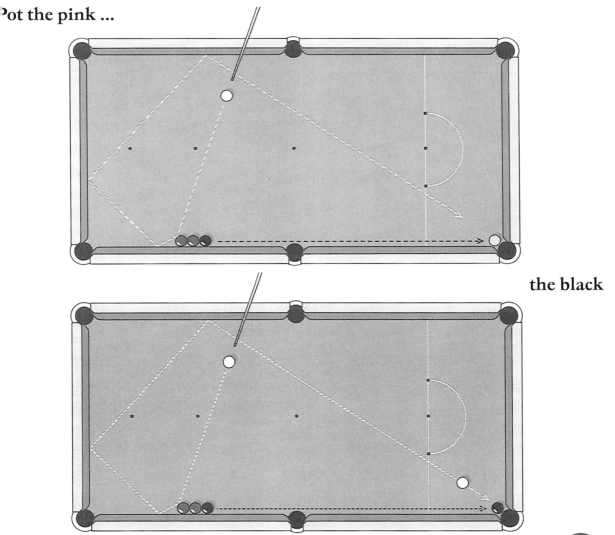

the black

THE HARDER THEY COME 96

If you thought Shot 94 was hard, you ain't seen nuthin' yet! This needs to be judged to perfection.

Two reds and the black are on the left side cushion, and you are going to pot the black in the middle left pocket.

Strike the cue ball at twelve o'clock and catch the end red thin. The black rolls up the cushion, and the white bounces off three sides and pots the black as it passes over the pocket.

All things are possible! Seriously, if the success rate wasn't that high with these shots, I wouldn't be doing them.

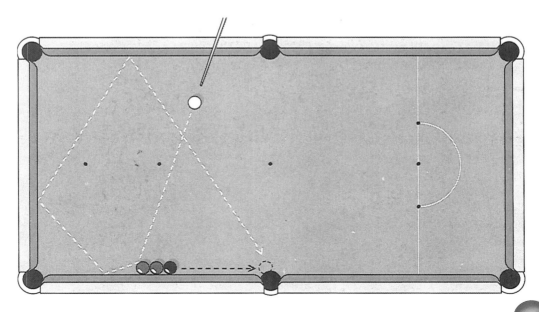

OH NO!
NOT THE BASKET

This one is very, very difficult. Put the black over the corner pocket. The basket facing the pocket diagonally opposite, and the pink and the cue ball in front of that. Pot the pink and black.

Strike the cue ball to pot the pink into the basket, the white then must jump over the basket and pot the black into the top pocket! You will be excused if you want to put a line of reds up near the top left pocket to make it easier. Then, if the white hits them, it might bounce onto the black.

This takes a lot of practice.

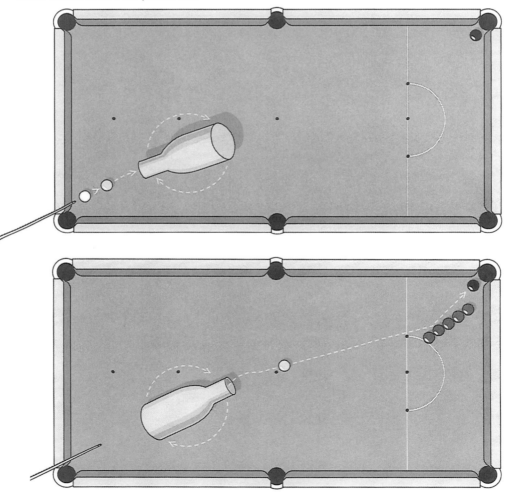

THE DUMB WAITER

Parental advice is sought before you try this for anyone under the age of 36! I have to include it because it's a classic shot but I wouldn't recommend anyone try it because even I have injured someone in the attempt.

Anyway, here it is ... Find a willing friend (suit of armour advisable) and get him to lie on the table with a square of chalk held between his teeth with the black ball placed on top. On top of the cushion is another square of chalk with the cue ball on.

Strike the cue ball into the air to hit the black out of the mouth and into the corner pocket. It's a great shot but the person lying on the table never sees it because they've always got their eyes closed!

A word of warning, check that your friend does not wear false teeth, otherwise they might pot too. Actually, come to think of it, that might be quite a spectacular shot ...

"I was in the snooker room of a hotel once and someone said, 'Why don't you play that shot where you knock the ball from someone's mouth?' I managed to persuade one of the kitchen porters to lie on the table, and I struck the cue ball and I hit him right on the chin! I then said, 'That's why I don't play it.'

In my trick shot video I used a tailors dummy but when I fluffed one attempt the ball made a great hole in his face!"

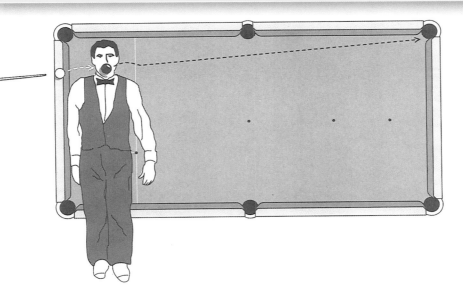

99 THREE, TWO, ONE

This is a shot I played successfully on *Big Break* but I think it's certainly one of the most difficult of all.

The green, brown and yellow are on their respective spots and the idea is to pot them in that order. But you are going to hit the yellow first, the brown second and the green last. No cue ball this time. Just strike the balls directly, each with increasing pace.

"The highlight of my career was definitely in 1979. In the April of that year I got to the semi-final of the World Championship but lost to Dennis Taylor. He was beaten in the final by Terry Griffiths. Five months later, in the United Kingdom Championship, I again played Dennis Taylor in the semi-final, beat him and met Terry Griffiths in the final – who was then the World Champion. I won the match but I was disappointed that I hadn't done that five months earlier because then I would have been the World Champion.

To have been United Kingdom champion is good. But it would have been nice to have said that I was World Champion. Anyway, I can't complain about snooker. It's given me a great life."

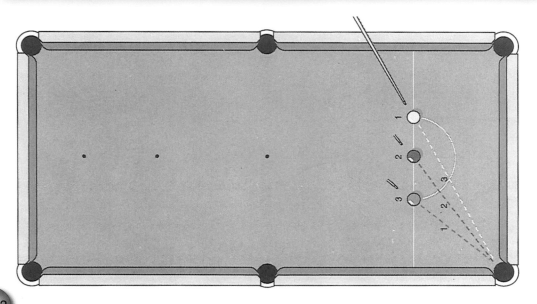